The Economics of U.S. Health Care Policy

Dr. Frank W. Musgrave is a professor of economics at Ithaca College where he has taught for thirty-eight years. Previously, he had taught social studies, including economics, at Lakewood Junior-Senior High School in Lakewood, New Jersey, for ten years. He is also the director of the Southern Tier (NY) Center for Economic Education at Ithaca College. He did his undergraduate study at Muhlenberg College; his graduate degrees (MBA, Ph.D.) are from Rutgers University, where he was a Walter Russell Scholar. Professor Musgrave is a distinguished fellow of the New York State Economics Association. He is a member of the International Honor Society in Economics, Omicron Delta Epsilon, and Phi Kappa Phi Honor Society. He has presented and published in the fields of health, labor, and education. Musgrave is married to Eva Mae Gifford Musgrave; they have two children, Marcia and Scott, and two grandchildren, Devon and Dylan. Eva Mae operates the Edge of Thyme Bed and Breakfast Inn in Candor, New York, where high tea is served upon appointment. Musgrave loves to travel and enjoys classical and jazz music as well as baseball. His basset hound, Winston, is a constant and loyal companion.

The Economics of U.S. Health Care Policy

The Role of Market Forces

Frank W. Musgrave

M.E.Sharpe
Armonk, New York
London, England

Copyright © 2006 by M.E. Sharpe, Inc.

All rights reserved. No part of this book may be reproduced in any form
without written permission from the publisher, M.E. Sharpe, Inc.,
80 Business Park Drive, Armonk, New York 10504.

Library of Congress Cataloging-in-Publication Data

Musgrave, Frank W., 1932–
  The economics of U.S. health care policy : the role of market forces /
Frank W. Musgrave.
    p. cm.
  Includes bibliographical references and index.
  ISBN 0-7656-1255-0 (hardcover : alk. paper)—ISBN 0-7656-1256-9 (pbk. : alk. paper)
  1. Medical policy. 2. Medical economics. 3. Medical care. I. Title:
Economics of US health care policy. II. Title.

RA395.A3M87 2006
362.1'0425—dc22   2005021725

Printed in the United States of America

The paper used in this publication meets the minimum requirements of
American National Standard for Information Sciences
Permanence of Paper for Printed Library Materials,
ANSI Z 39.48-1984.

♾

MV (c)   10   9   8   7   6   5   4   3   2   1
MV (p)   10   9   8   7   6   5   4   3   2   1

To Eva Mae Gifford Musgrave, my love and real life line

and

Monroe Berkowitz, my mentor and academic life line.

Contents

List of Tables and Figures

Tables

Figures

Preface

This book examines the viability and the limits of health care services delivered as either public goods or private goods. That is, what are the trade-offs as nations pursue additional funding needs for health care? Does public funding of health care expenditures limit the availability of certain services at the time consumers want them? Does private funding limit access to health care services for low-income people? The notion of exploring a number of contemporary health care issues to address these questions grew out of an increasing interest in applied economics and its use as an analytical tool.

As the manuscript moved to the production phase, some significant issues surfaced in the news that appear to reveal limits to both the public good and private good approaches. For the Quebec province, the Supreme Court of Canada declared that nationalized insurance no longer had a monopoly. Since the national insurance plan was unable or unwilling to meet all the needs of the public, there was a complementary role for private insurance that had been previously banned. Private health care facilities are now developing in China, some in cooperation with the government. Meanwhile, in the United States, there has been a revised interest in universal health care in the form of single-payer (government) systems. Although universal health care has been proposed and already rejected in some states, private insurance is unable to accommodate the growing ranks of the medically uninsured or underinsured. Some states are revising their Medicaid program (federal-state medical program for low-income people) to allow consumer-directed varying individual uses of the funds. All of these events seem to confirm the thesis of this book.

That is, the expansion of health care services beyond the constraints of public budgets ultimately requires either private resources or private insurance. Conversely, the private sector has responded well to the demand for expanded health care services; however, this has only exacerbated access issues for the elderly and the poor. Hence, we see expansion of public funding in the United States of pharmaceutical products for the elderly.

This book provides the theoretical and empirical research findings that suggest intelligent mixes of public and private health care services. When the findings are applied to the several issues central to the U.S. health care, we may be able to forge policies that are efficient, efficacious and equitable. Elimination or benign neglect of the extreme policy proposals may have to precede this possibility.

September 2005
Ithaca, New York

Acknowledgments

My wife, Eva Mae, has remained steadfast with love through a few action-packed and stressful years during my preparation of this manuscript. She also rescued me from certain disaster in my attempts at surviving computer reality.

Tina Bennett, administrative assistant at Ithaca College, was able to decipher my scribblings and transform them to efficiently word processed documents. She did her work tirelessly and effectively with great patience. A number of students provided able assistance. Thomas Cole identified most of the necessary data, journal articles and books for this project. Victoria Besner provided additional sources and an updating of research materials. Ashley Parmarter organized the materials into separate files and then prepared the bibliography.

Jim Bondra, research librarian at Ithaca College, provided invaluable assistance in identifying and accessing electronic government data. Fred Estabrook, Manager of Graphic Design Services, provided the graphs for some of the figures and tables. He did them well even under a time constraint.

The editorial staff at M.E. Sharpe have been very helpful and supportive. Executive Editor Lynn Taylor has patiently witnessed the coming and going of deadlines. She has shepherded the preparation and processing of the manuscript in an efficacious manner. Amanda Allensworth has been pleasant and prompt in responding to my questions. My thanks to Angela Piliouras for her capable work as production editor. Susanna Sharpe did well with the unenviable task of copyediting.

Dean Howard Erlich of the School of Humanities and Sciences at Ithaca College was the enabler for my sabbatical leave. Judith Kip was the outside professional who did the indexing. Many thanks to all. Any remaining errors or omissions may be rightfully charged to the author.

The Economics of U.S. Health Care Policy

1

Introduction

Health Care Choices, Trade-Offs, and Ownership of Health Care Resources

As a fool is about to dive into a pool of shallow water, an economist says in a whispered voice, "Someone is going to get hurt!" When the fool completes his dive by hitting his head on the concrete bottom of the pool, the economist shouts, "I told you so!"

Life is full of choices, costs, and trade-offs. To complicate matters, we want to have some control over our lives, the ability to have some say, or empowerment of the resources that we own, for example, human resources and those resources that affect us. This command of resources is a central issue in health care policies today. Do we want government to be in command of all health care decisions, that is, as a single buyer of all health care with a global budget that determines what, how, how much, when, and for whom health care services are produced? The economist would likely say, "You can take that path, but I will tell you what it will cost you." There are trade-offs. The National Health Service (NHS) in the United Kingdom is an example of a socialized, or nationalized, health care system. In 1999, the NHS spent 450 million pounds (about $792 million) on contracts with private health care providers at competitive prices. Additionally, some NHS physicians are taking private patients in NHS hospitals for extra fees paid by NHS. Tony Blair, the prime minister, indicated that he had "absolutely no ideological problem" with these arrangements (Rogers 2000, p. 2). In other words, the U.K. government is the producer with the NHS hospitals and physicians (state operated and employed) and the provider of services through private contractors. This is explicit recognition of the inherent rationing of services in a nationalized system that has a budget constraint. However, in this situation the United Kingdom has allowed the underutilized private system to complement the constrained public system in order to accommodate the demand for health care services. This adjustment by the U.K. nationalized system is evidence of emphasis on access to health care with an acknowledgment of a private system's ability to respond to consumer demand. Some in the United Kingdom are suggesting that their system is modeled like the former Soviet command economy, which was inefficient and not responsive to consumers. One of these critics, David Smith, suggests that "patients should have a price on their heads, and GPs [general practitioners] should compete to retain or attract them. The more explicit the fee, the more the new GP practices would be encouraged to move into the market and compete aggressively for patients" (Smith 2000, p. 6).

What does all of this have to say about choices, costs, and command of health care resources? Do we choose a nationalized health care system with a global budget and a single payer (the U.K. model)? If so, we are assured of financial access to services but are denied the choice of kinds and amounts of medical services, products, and providers that would be integral to a private market system. The market could spur a better connection between supplier decisions and preferences of consumers for a menu of medical services at prices they are willing to pay. Indeed, the purpose of markets, operating on a competitive basis, is to allocate scarce resources to their most productive (efficient) and desired uses. So, while nationalized systems emphasize equality or fairness in the form of access to services via a single payer with a global budget (one source-government), market-based systems emphasize responsiveness to consumer needs with financial incentives to suppliers. The market system engenders consumer choices predicated on individual preferences and constrained by prices and incomes. Perhaps, one consumer would prefer spending more on nutrition and exercise; a different consumer would prefer to forgo some current consumption on health care in order to save for the possibility of the need for long-term care; another consumer would prefer a variety of paraprofessional and electronic sources for health care, and so on. Theoretically, this market system, if competitive, would direct suppliers to produce services that consumers demand at the lowest possible cost in order to continue supplying the services with a resultant profit or surplus. The United States has the highest portion (over 50 percent) of health care expenditures that are privately funded compared to all other major industrialized countries (see Table 1.1 in the next section of this chapter). The United States produces over 50 percent of new pharmaceutical products and has the highest percentage (14 percent) of the gross domestic product (GDP) devoted to health care expenditures. In other words, consumers want to spend more on health care and they get more health care. Thus, the market system reflects consumer priorities and encourages more diverse and productive responses from suppliers of health care. However, just as the nationalized systems seek ways to satisfy consumer demand that gets rationed, market systems face the need to provide more access, particularly in the form of additional or universal insurance coverage. There are major gaps in the United States for the medically underinsured and the uninsured. Employers, faced with increasing premiums for employee health insurance benefits, have been reducing benefits for employees and increasing the share of costs borne by employees. Some small businesses have stopped all health insurance coverage for their employees. Some young adults have forgone insurance coverage. This topic will be covered more completely in Chapter 5, on the uninsured.

Early in 2004, the Institute of Medicine publicly issued a report recommending universal health insurance coverage in the United States by the year 2010. The report indicates that 43 million Americans are uninsured, including 8.5 million children (Institute of Medicine 2004, pp. 1–3). The government role would be to require coverage for everyone with vouchers, or tax credits for low-income families or individuals. The insurance would be through private insurance companies with government oversight. This universal coverage for insurance should not be confused with universal care with nationalized insurance. The latter in Canada has caused considerable trade-offs in the form of long queues for some surgeries such as heart bypass surgery, even to the extent of waiting in hospital corridors for hours or days and, sometimes, having the surgery in the corridor. When forced to operate at capacity to accommodate patients, the Canadian system rations care in the form of deciding who on the long list for surgery will fill the allotted surgical times for the day (Cherney 2003, p. 1). Thus, the United States has few waiting or queue problems but, as indicated previously, there are many who lack the financial means or the insurance coverage for health care. The Canadians have universal and nationalized insurance coverage but face the rationing of long waits. Another model of health care is a nationalized or socialized health care system where most of the care is extended through public (state owned and operated) hospitals and physicians and other professional staff who are state employees. This model of health care, or variations of it, is present in the United Kingdom, Australia, Italy, and Sweden. In these nationalized systems, there are also considerable waiting times for elective surgery. The United Kingdom has also experienced considerable loss of health care professionals to positions in the United States where pay is higher and the available state-of-the-art technology is attractive. Thus, even when nationalized systems are present, health care is not always available when and where patients seek it.

The Uniqueness of the Health Care Industry (Sector)

There are many features of health care that are unique with respect to institutional framework, role of government, and market initiatives. Although these differences are present in health care systems in many nations of the world, they are very evident and pronounced in the United States. We find that some of these features are being challenged by an ever-evolving system with more emphasis on market forces and institutional change than on government micromanagement. These features include:

- asymmetry of information
- the public-good nature of health care
- the inverse relationship between public funding and shares of GDP for health care services
- heavy regulation of the health care industry
- third-party influences

Asymmetry of Information

For markets to work well, even under competitive conditions, there must be information available to both buyers and sellers. However, in health care markets, there are pronounced differences between buyers and sellers with respect to possession of information. This asymmetry is clearly in favor of the providers of health care, that is, the physicians, hospitals, pharmaceutical companies, and the financiers of health care including insurance companies, pharmacy benefit managers, health maintenance organizations (HMOs), preferred provider organizations (PPOs), and managed care companies. This imbalance of information allows prices for health care to be set independently of the values that consumers place on health care services and the quantity demanded of those services. Therefore, prices cannot act fully in accord with consumer preferences, nor can consumer preferences act as a discipline on providers' prices.

The Public-Good Nature of Health Care

The extent to which health care is viewed as a public good depends, in part, on the success of market-oriented systems relative to the success of government as a provider/producer/financier. Market directions in health care reform have taken place in many countries that had previously been examples of government-managed or nationalized systems. In Chapter 2 there is more extensive discussion of these matters. Suffice it to say that there is agreement that health care is a public good, but major disagreement on whether the government or the market should be the allocator of health care services. In many European countries, government-managed or nationalized health care systems have looked to the market for efficiency-based reforms while holding on to the role of the government in assuring equity, including financial access and macromanagement of payment systems. In contrast, the United States is looking to national (federal) direction to solve the problems of the uninsured and the underinsured as well as national assistance for seniors in the procurement of pharmaceutical products. Some of the public goods in the United States are really quasi-public goods, as in the case of Medicare (federal program of health insurance for older Americans). Medicare is a price-excludable public good since seniors must pay the first part of their hospital care as a deductible. Therefore, many low-income people consider this deductible as a barrier to health care; some low-income people are excluded from receiving some health care. The public-good nature of health care is evident in the heavy regulation of the industry.

The Inverse Relationship Between Public Funding and Shares of GDP for Health Care Services

For most of the advanced nations of the world, as the percentage of GDP devoted to health care expenditures rises, the percentage of public funding (as opposed to private funding) of health care expenditures falls. The converse holds as well. This is illustrated in Table 1.1. This inverse relationship may be attributable to the constraining effects of governments that assume major and increasing shares of the financing of health care services. These constraints take the form of placing limits on the quantity, types, and availability of health care services. In contrast, those countries that have relatively less government spending enjoy a greater responsiveness to their expressed demand for more health care services

Table 1.1

Health Care Expenditures and Public Funding

Country	Health care expenditures as percentage of GDP		Percentage of health care expenditures as publicly funded	
	1998	2001	1998	2001
United States	12.9	13.9	44.84	44.4
Canada	9.3	9.7	70.17	70.8
France	9.4	9.5	77.7	76.0
Japan	7.4	7.6*	78.5	78.3*
United Kingdom	6.8	7.6	83.3	82.2

Source: OECD, *Health at a Glance* (2001, pp. 43–45, and 2003b, pp. 121, 127).
* Data for 2000

and delivery of those services in a timely manner. The United States, with its majority of health care expenditures emanating from the private sector, affords us with a superb example of differences as compared with other advanced nations.

The simple model would posit government as a single buyer of health care services with a global budget. One could expect that when this global budget was exhausted, within a fiscal period of time, all financial provision of health care would end. Up to that point in time, patients could get care if it was available and if all of the patients were not too far back in the queue.

This simple model tells the basic story. However, in systems where the government is the major, but not only, funder of health care services, there are other trade-offs. The banners which proclaim "Affordable Health Care for All" or "Universal Health Care" either express support of the simple model or the supporters of the banners are blithely unaware of the adverse consequences or trade-offs. The publicly funded systems (over 70-plus percent of health care expenditures publicly funded) have experienced a number of difficulties, particularly for the intended beneficiaries. These systems have experienced a relative disadvantage as far as technological advances in medical care compared to the more privately funded system. The use of more intensive procedures is far greater in the United States than in other countries. For example, the United States has a much higher rate of heart bypass surgery than Canada, which uses more of the less intensive angioplasty (Cutler 2002, pp. 892–894). While there is no clear evidence that the use of more intensive procedures results in lower rates of morbidity or mortality, the contrast is that the consumer and physician have a greater choice and that they are not constrained by a government-financed one-size-fits-all menu of services.

The United Kingdom's national health service sets very restrictive limits on the availability of kidney dialysis for end-stage renal failure patients. Given a national budget and a fixed number of kidney dialysis centers, there is an explicit rationing system operative in the United Kingdom. In recent years, only three out of one million patients between the ages of sixty-five and seventy-five who were diagnosed as in need of kidney dialysis were able to receive the treatment. For diagnosed patients over the age of seventy-five, *none* received kidney dialysis. With a limited number of centers and stations, the Brits have made a conscious decision to ration kidney dialysis in favor of younger people and to the inevitable decrease in survival rates of the elderly.

Among the advanced nations of the world, the United States is the sole nation that has most of its health care financed privately (over 50 percent). However, the public share has increased slightly in recent years. This may represent a trend, especially with the major public expenditures expected with the impact of the Medicare Modernization Act (MMA) of 2003. Within the MMA is a large entitlement program of pharmaceutical drugs for people over the age of sixty-five (see Chapter 7, on Medicare reform). It is estimated that approximately 20 to 25 percent of pharmaceutical drugs will be publicly funded. There may be additional expenditures on these drugs that are influenced by the new program. The significance of the new program may be in its influence on the quantity, types, and timely availability of these drugs. The American government is developing a formulary that will specify which drugs are covered. In other words, the government is constrained politically by its budget. Certainly, the seniors and pharmaceutical companies want a larger list of drugs from which to choose. This U.S. government determined or approved formulating shares the practice of the European countries, which places limits on the quantity, types, and availability of drugs for consumers. Hence, the separation of the consumer and the physician from the choices implicit in a market-driven system is apparent. In the other advanced countries, there are a number of examples of limitations on quantity, types, and availability of pharmaceutical drugs born of the constraints of public budgets. The inverse relationship, as illustrated in Table 1.1, between the percentage of a nation's GDP that is spent on health care expenditures and the percentage of health care expenditures that are publicly funded has its manifestation in those limitations. Dr. David Gratzer, senior fellow at the Manhattan Institute, offers the following examples:

1. Ninety percent of patients in France with acute asthma are given the necessary drug therapy only on an ad hoc basis rather than on a regular basis.
2. Over 80 percent of Italian patients in need of cholesterol-reducing statins do not obtain these drugs.
3. In the province of Ontario, Canada, the government finances over 40 percent of the prescription drug expenditures. In Germany, the government share is 70 percent. One can understand, if not appreciate, how these public finance budget constraints limit the amount, types, and availability of pharmaceutical budgets.
4. In the United States, Medicare reimbursement for physician services is set by a government scale called a Relative Value Resource Based Scale (RVRBS). The lack of market mechanisms or a managed care organization (MCO) providing a negotiated market price often results in a price paid to physicians that is less than the value of their services. This means that many physicians do not accept Medicare patients. Hence, there is a limit on availability of services (Gratzer 2003, on-line pages).

Heavy Regulation of the Health Care Industry

A typical U.S. hospital may face as many as three to four hundred federal, state, regional, and local agencies and regulators within a year's time. These regulations can impede competition and efficiency, although few would argue that many of the regulations are not necessary.

Third-Party Influences

Over 85 percent of hospital care is financed by a third party, that is, a party other than the buyer or seller of hospital services. Third parties include insurance companies, government, HMOs, and managed care companies. This financing influence separates the services that consumers purchase from their financial responsibility; therefore, the moral hazard that consumers will demand more health care services than they may actually need or even want increases. On the other hand, the provider may not be able to exercise professional responsibility or have autonomy of decision making with the presence of managed care. Further, the government-subsidized and tax-preference treatment for health insurance may lead to more health insurance and more health care, albeit with inflationary effects.

The Bi-Modal Structure of the Hospital Industry

For the most part in the United States, hospitals are not-for-profit private corporations. These hospitals compete for patients within their service areas, which tend to overlap with service areas of other hospitals. Most of these hospitals are now in "negotiated markets," which means that they enter contracts with third-party payers such as Blue Cross, HMOs, PPOs, MCOs, and others for the rate at which they will be reimbursed or paid at point-of-service (POS). By the late 1990s, all states in the United States ended their management and control of reimbursement rates. Consequently, hospitals negotiated with the third parties for rates of reimbursement. This produced efficiencies that became the hallmark of managed care.

In contrast, in some large cities, large investor-owned for-profit hospitals and hospital chains (horizontally integrated) have developed major shares of hospital market. This has resulted in monopoly pricing power that clearly subdues the managed care competitive pricing characteristic of most hospitals. In other words, these for-profit hospitals can price their services above the competitive norms and realize what economists call "rents," payments above the value of the services rendered.

Major Gaps in the Insurance System

1. About 44 million Americans were medically uninsured in 2002.

2. Medicare, the U.S. system of medical and hospital insurance for the elderly, is facing dwindling reserves and increasing costs for its benefits program. Medicare requires its beneficiaries to pay the first $900 in 2005 for hospital care along with a number of co-payments. These requirements present barriers to health care for low-income seniors. Medicare beneficiaries, under the Medicare Modernization Act (MMA) of 2003, now have some coverage for pharmaceutical products. The program requires some out-of-pocket payments that are capped. The provi-

sions of the new law are implemented in stages that began with a drug discount card in 2004. The program will be fully discussed in Chapter 7. This new law reflects the unique nature of the American health care system. This system maintains and ensures competitive markets, private insurance, and private pricing (without controls) of drugs as well as some government provision for benefits. There will be joint financing of the program by Medicare beneficiaries, taxpayers, third-party payers, employers, and employees. The new law provides subsidies and tax credits to encourage full implementation of the coverage. The United States, alone among major countries, prefers use of private markets to provide efficiency in resource use with the government "filling the gaps" and providing greater financial access to the system. The reform of Medicare will encourage individual responsibility for those people under the age of sixty-five with the use of health savings accounts (HSAs). These accounts combine a high-deductible medical insurance policy with a tax-advantaged savings account that would assist in the financing of the deductible amounts. The high-deductible accounts have relatively low premiums that help in the financing of health care. The new program would continue to move Americans away from entitlements and increase the uniqueness of the system.

3. There exists the problem of the medically *under*insured. With rising costs of insurance premiums, employers have asked for more contributions from employees and have reduced their coverage.

4. Medicaid, the federal/state/local-county insurance program for low-income people, has become a tax issue as local and/or county governments struggle to pay their shares of the rising costs of the program. With many states already in fiscal crisis, the pressure to maintain Medicaid has resulted in significant increases in local and county property taxes.

All of the major gaps in U.S. health insurance coverage have increased the pressure on the federal government to reconsider the feasibility of universal health insurance.

The Unique Nature of the Demand for Health Care

Consumers do not have a *per se* demand for health care but rather want health care as an alternative to pain. In general, this leads to a relatively low price elasticity of demand for health care. This low price elasticity is compounded by the asymmetry of information characteristic of health care mentioned earlier. However, the increasing awareness of consumers to health care issues is being assisted by new access to information via the Internet and by alternative paths to health care such as better information on diet, exercise, nutrition, and healthy lifestyles.

A Unique Institutional Arrangement in which the Prices Paid by Consumers Are Separately Determined from the Prices that Sellers of Health Care Agree to Accept

The out-of-pocket prices that consumers pay (deductibles, co-payments, etc.) disguise the total price, much of which is paid by third parties. The sellers are often in "take-it-or-leave-it" managed care markets where either they agree to participate in the negotiated price arrangement or do not enter the system at all. In other words, consumers are paying prices through contracts with employees and managed care/point-of-service arrangements. On the other hand, providers of health services are accepting payment for their services that is *not* necessarily equal to the value that consumers place on their services. In order to have efficiency in markets, there has to be a connection between what the supplier needs to receive to cover his/her costs, including implicit costs, and the amount the consumer is willing and able to pay. Health care markets, in general, do not allow for this connection; therefore, there is widespread inefficiency. Exceptions such as medical savings accounts, individual/group brokers, and discount cards or buyers' clubs do allow for more efficiency.

In the next chapter, the policy menu will be placed into the context of the important conceptual issues necessary to provide an economic analysis. In a sense, this will abstract from a policy perspective such that attention can be gathered to some fundamental issues and concepts. Economics will be examined in definition and in the nature of the economizing problem. The basic questions will be posed of what, how, how much, when, and for whom health care is produced. And, of course, who pays? These questions are at the very foundation of every health care issue. The choice of answering mechanisms will determine whether it is the market, a government command center, or hybrids that will set the stage for the ultimate mix of public, quasi-public, and private goods. After a primer on pricing and how this is applied to health care services and products, there will be a series of chapters on issues including pharmaceutical pricing, managed care, the uninsured, medical (or health) savings accounts, and the penultimate chapter on Medicare reform. Medicare reform encompasses all of the perviously mentioned issues and the need to delineate the lines of responsibility for the delivery and financing of health care. One of the major contributions of this reform of Medicare is to set forth all of the constituents of health care and to ask the ultimate questions, as posed in the final chapter. These questions will include: Who is in command of our health care resources, who pays, and are there appropriate and separate roles for the M.D., the consumer, the business firm, and the government? Is there a possibility of convergence of health care financing programs in the world? Do we all need to allow for government to provide equity and access? Do we all need to promote efficiency (economizing on scarce health resources) and consumer choice?

2

The Mix of Health Services

More Market and More Government?

The Setting

Nothing could be more timely and at the heart of our concerns about our health care services than the December 2003 reform of Medicare. This new program not only directly affects senior citizens in their quest for financial assistance for the buying of pharmaceutical products, but also attempts to set the mix of government and market roles for health care services in a new and evolving relationship. The new government support for seniors has developed not only a new entitlement benefit but also a very significant role for private insurance and for competitive markets for the economy and even for people under the age of sixty-five. In particular, health savings accounts (a form of the more generic term, medical savings accounts) will encourage people to develop savings habits through the use of these accounts so that they will be able to command their own resources in the purchase of health care services. Call it consumer sovereignty or the ability to make individual choices and to be individually responsible. These health savings accounts will be accompanied by high-deductible major medical insurance policies which have relatively low premiums. Health savings accounts and medical savings accounts will be covered in Chapter 6. The current chapter sorts out the perceived problems in our current system and sets forth the important economic concepts, definitions, and norms in order to provide an economic analysis of the important questions facing Americans. We need to look at some numbers to get an objective measurement of our system. Our health care system looks at government as the access agent for care for the elderly, the uninsured, and the lower-income consumers. Other nations use private sources to access demand for a limited quantity of nationalized hospital beds and health care professionals.

Perhaps the health care systems of the world are on a convergence path. The government is the agent of access and fairness and the market is the agent of choice and of economizing our scarce health care resources.

The Problem

There appears to be a national consensus that health care expenditures are increasing at an alarming rate and are much higher than in other countries. Even with the price-deflating effects of managed care, the medical care component of the consumer price index increased 4.9 percent from the third quarter of 2001 to the third quarter of 2002 while the overall consumer price index increased only 1.5 percent for the same period of time (MB Inflation Monitor 2002, p. 5). Consumers have benefited from lower prices through managed care but recently have resisted the effects of restricted benefits and limited choice of the program. This resistance has manifested itself in more choices for both physicians and consumers along with higher prices. This is evidence of trade-offs in health care policies. The increases in health care expenditures have outpaced the growth of GDP in recent years. For example, health care expenditures increased to $1.6 trillion in 2002, representing an increase of 9.3 percent over the year 2001. At the same time, health care spending as a percentage of GDP rose to 14.9 percent (Levit et al. 2004, p. 147).

Before we become too alarmed about all of this, we should keep in mind a few general observations. First, since Americans make decisions in the marketplace, we may simply be exercising our freedom in demanding more health care products and services relative to other goods and services. Moreover, most of us have real increases in our incomes and are better able to purchase these services that have become available. We are willing and able to purchase health care. Second, health care expenditures are a function of price times quantity. If prices were to remain constant and if there were no increase in the number or quality of health care services available to consumers, we might still face increases in health care expenditures. That is, an increase in the number of consumers each paying the same prices for the same number of goods and services purchased would result in an increase of health care expenditures. In economic jargon, there would be a horizontal summation of a greater number of individual demand functions. That is, there would be an increase in demand that would result in higher prices, assuming all other factors remained constant. If we add other demographic factors, we might have a further clue to increasing expenditures. The over-sixty-five age cohort is growing larger relative to other age cohorts in the population and its constituents are living longer. This segment of the population consumes a disproportional share of pharmaceutical products (details to follow in Chapter 3, on pharmaceutical pricing). If there is an increasing number of new products and services, and if more people use these services more often, there will be even greater positive effects on prices. The marketing of all kinds of services and products has become more aggressive. Consumer awareness of health and new products has led to more expenditures on health care services. Other factors include the effects of overall increases in prices for products and services that health care providers purchase. The effects of third-party payers—including insurance companies, managed care organizations, and government—in lowering out-of-pocket expenses are of major significance. In some hospital service areas, investor-owned for-profit hospitals control major shares of the market and can ignore the managed care influences of more competitively structured markets. That is, these hospital chains can exert monopoly pricing power and extract rents, which are profits well above the value of services provided and would be present under competitive forces. As indicated in Chapter 1, there are a number of unique features about our health services sector that contribute to the trends of increasing expenditures.

The sheer number of medically uninsured people in the United States, about 42 million in 2002, is of major concern, as is the related problem of limited access to health care for low-income individuals and families. On a less discernible basis, there appears a growing perception that it ought to be easier to get health care and to pay for it; Canadians seem to have an "easier" system. A corollary of this perception is that the quest for equity and efficacy is greater than the quest for efficiency. Moreover, even though efficacy, efficiency, and equity may not be mutually exclusive, the immediate drive for one may adversely affect the others. That is, if we perceive the need for a greater number of people to be insured, greater access to the system for low-income consumers and for administrative ease (less paperwork and bureaucracy), then we may expect some trade-offs between this relative push for efficacy and equity and our quest for efficiency. Efficiency would come in the terms of allocation of scarce health care resources to their most productive and desired uses. To put it more simply, a greater access and insurance coverage for the population may cost us more than we are willing tolerate in the form of increased insurance premiums, private health care costs, or higher taxes. If the government finances increases in health care coverage with a payroll tax, we can expect a shifting of the burden of taxes to the middle- and low-income taxpayers. On the other hand, if we succeed in containing costs (more cost-effective), we will have to ration health care. This will mean our consumers will have less health care at any point in time.

The trade-off between equity and efficiency has taken on much more in policy considerations over the past four decades. Access to the system, particularly in the form of uniform health insurance, was the paramount goal as nations began to develop health systems. This equity or sense of equality overshadowed any real concerns about costs of health care. More recently, with health care expenditures expanding in an absolute sense and as a share of GDP, efficiency and cost-containment issues have dominated government policy concerns (Cutler 2002, pp. 881–882). According to David Cutler, "the result of this technological change is that governments face increasingly severe financing crises. Many countries can no longer afford the commitment to complete equality that they once could" (2002, pp. 881–882). Governments began to use a number of regulatory controls on costs and revenues for providers, and they reviewed requests for use of technology. The results of these controls were mixed but generally encouraged inefficiency and penalized efficiency. In the United States, many states developed per diem payments by third parties (insurance, government) that appeared to pay more to those hospitals that have longer average lengths of stay than those hospitals that promoted earlier exits and more ambulatory services. More recently, managed care became the vehicle of choice in place of state insurance offices as the broker between buyers and sellers of health care services in the United States. Managed care organizations (MCOs) are mainly forms of health maintenance organizations (HMOs) and preferred provider organizations (PPOs) that negotiate discounted health care prices with health care providers for employees of firms who enroll in the MCO or insurance carrier. These MCOs have reduced many of the inefficiencies in our health care system and have established the importance of efficiency in all countries that face increasing demand for health care services. However, most governments realize their mission of providing the equity may be endangered as health care delivery becomes more efficient. Later in this chapter, we will examine the options for nations that wish to combine the virtues of equity and efficiency in health care reform. First, the next section develops some norms and definitions.

The Mix: Public and Private Goods

Since this book is really a study of the mix of public and private goods in health care systems, it behooves us to define the norms of efficiency and equity. In general, we posit that the United States presumes that market mechanisms direct consumer choices and producer initiatives to their most productive and desired uses. In most other nations, the presumption is that the government should direct health care resources in a redistributive and reallocative manner to those who have the least ability to command health care services. That is, the burden of change would fall on those who offer policies that would contradict or ignore these presumptions.

In a pragmatic manner, many countries have shrugged off the policy constraints that these presumptions imply. Rather than either public goods or private goods, most nations have allowed markets and governments to use their complementary roles in the pursuit of production of a sustainable and affordable amount of health care services. The U.S. government has extended public provision of pharmaceutical drugs for people over the age of sixty-five. This has required a formulary that specifies the types and quantities of drugs that will be financed by the government. Greater access to and financing of these drugs will necessarily limit the choices and availability under market- or consumer-directed care. Conversely, there are a number of nationalized or government-controlled plans that have been forced by limited government funds to seek more directions by market demand and consumer choices. We have cited some of these examples in Chapter 1. These policy paradigms are conditioned by issues of equity that are of major concern to countries with nationalized or regulated health care systems. Will consumers have the financial means to obtain health care services? Will the government provide these services directly or will government effect a distribution or redistribution of these services such that there is little, if any, out-of-pocket expense to the consumer? In other words, are health care services nonexclusive and nondistributive? Further, if government budgets are inadequate to support this public role, will governments solicit assistance from private sources? If the answers to these questions are all "yes," then public goods become necessary, but only necessary *and* sufficient with the addition of some private produced or provided goods and services. The use of market or market-like mechanisms by a nationalized system also serves the goals of equity and access. That is, the market mechanisms tend to economize on relatively scarce (expensive) resources, thus producing a greater availability of health care services.

The United Kingdom has used internal market-like mechanisms such as allowing doctors and hospitals the use of funds to do their own shopping for the resources they need and that fit the needs of the public they serve. The result is that the U.K. has been able to provide services more economically while holding to the national goals of access and equity. In other words, it is easier to provide an adequate supply of nationalized health care services in an era of rapidly rising costs if market mechanisms can remove some of the inefficiencies in the system. Conversely, the United States has the lowest percentage of health care services that are publicly funded. The Medicare system for the elderly had consistently lacked coverage for one of the largest expenditure categories, pharmaceutical drugs. With the Medicare reform of 2003, pharmaceutical coverage (with limitations and co-payments) fills part of this gap. However, the U.S. program has relied on private insurance companies and private, unregulated pharmaceutical companies to provide the financing and provision of these drugs. Also, in the United States there is a major initiative of consumer-directed health coverage that combines individually brokered services with health savings accounts (HSAs) to develop consumer choice and preferences.

In order to sort out policy options for nations in the financing and provision of health care services, the following section develops a set of norms, definitions, conditions, and bases as a guide and common ground for the analyses that follow in this and other chapters.

The Norms, Definitions, Conditions, and Bases for Public Policy Decisions

In order for informed consent to give rise to an effective, equitable, and efficacious health care policy, the "body politic" needs agreement on norms and definitions. What is efficiency? What is equity? How is equity affected by efficiency? Are there trade-offs between these terms? Are the benefits of the health care system worth the cost? Part of the answers to these questions will depend on the appetites of government and the governed for market- or consumer-directed health care relative to nationalized or regulated health care. A positive or pure economic analysis will produce a rational basis for public policy choices and the likely trade-offs. If we regulate more, might there be a limitation of choices and quantities? If we depend on markets, will there be less access to the system? In order to address these questions, we will need to agree on the definitions and norms.

Efficiency has been defined in a number of ways that include the use of abstract concepts and quantitative measures. For the purposes of this book, we will use more generalized definitions. *Allocative efficiency* is attained when relatively scarce resources are channeled to their most desired (consumer utility) and most productive uses. *Technological efficiency* is attained when a given amount of a good or service is produced at the lowest-cost combination of the resources used in the production. Any increase in the ratio of output to dollar cost of inputs for a particular good or service would measure a gain in productivity. Productivity increases can reduce inflationary effects of wage increases by lowering per-unit costs of labor.

There are several other definitions and criteria for efficiency. These criteria are demanding as disciplinarians and require competitive markets in order to produce the desired results. Efficiency obtains when a consumer gets as much extra satisfaction per dollar expended on an additional amount of health care as she does per dollar expended for other goods and services. This would be the combination of health care and other goods and services that maximizes her utility (satisfaction) from health care within her budget constraint. Under competitive market conditions, the consumer would be willing to pay a price for an additional unit of health care services at exactly the extra cost incurred by the provider of health care services for that additional unit. These costs for the producer or provider include the usual or explicit costs of production *and* the implicit costs. The implicit costs used in economic analysis are costs incurred in forgoing alternative uses with higher returns. Private insurance companies may be bribed by Medicare to cover people with greater incidences of high risk (Landers 2003b, on-line pages). Under competitive market conditions, efficiency moves from abstract concepts to concrete outcomes. These results are confirmed on a daily basis and over time in market economies. Efficiency leads to lower prices, higher output, lower costs of production, and more choices. These prices reflect both the consumer's relative preferences for goods and services and the producer's willingness to provide for those preferences. Consumers would differ in the selections of what goods and services they would put in their "market baskets." Thus, choices are very real and viable. Even though we are not blessed with perfectly competitive markets, the results of efficiency are more attainable as the level of competition increases.

This framework for analysis of health care issues allows us to evaluate the role of private insurers in the coverage of pharmaceutical drugs under the provisions of the Medicare Modernization Act of 2003. This act also provided for a form of ownership accounts called health savings accounts (HSAs) that will allow consumers to direct choices for health care within the deductible amounts of their health insurance plans (see Chapters 6 and 7, on HSAs and Medicare reform). The market will be tested as a viable mechanism to offer competitive prices and inducements to save. The requirement of competitive markets for efficiency outcomes is a constant theme throughout this book. It is significant if only to suggest that anti-trust enforcement has a role to play in keeping markets competitive. We will see this role in the context of alternative government schemes in the financing of health care. If markets are not competitive, government agencies have been lured to administering prices to achieve reimbursement rates that reflect efforts to contain costs of health care. The alternative is to have private markets negotiate prices in the form of managed care. The enemies of competitive pricing are the monopolies or oligopolies that control some major urban markets. This control that has been exercised by investor-owned private for-profit hospital chains allows these firms to ignore the managed care organizations and to do their own form of administered pricing (see Chapter 4, on managed care). The role for anti-trust action in this environment appears to be obvious. Externalities, market failure, and rents present in the market system may induce public intervention. We will discuss these issues later in this chapter when we define public goods.

Equity and *efficacy* represent other possible paradigms for health care policies. Equity may be defined as being sensitive to the needs of people in societies who lack adequate access to health care. Equity raises distributional questions that challenge the concept that more efficient systems produce the most health care for all. A "rising tide lifts all ships" philosophy or strategy would support the efficiency argument. The distribution or redistribution would be ranked second to the need for efficiency. "Affordable health care for all" might require equal access to and availability of health care for all regardless of the ability to pay for the care. Global, single-payer, or nationalized systems that require little, if any, out-of-pocket expenses from citizens are the political forms of equity. Some would argue that equity in health care is a noble goal and attainable if its costs of delivery are affordable.

Early in the history of health care systems, efficiency was not much of a concern since equity could be financed at a relatively low cost. However, as health care services became more extensively used with the advent of new forms of care and technology, attention was drawn to efficiency (Cutler 2002, pp. 881–882). Health systems needed to find ways to manage costs in order to finance increasing numbers of consumers demanding access to an extended list of health care services. In Chapter 4, we analyze the various government attempts at efficiency in the United States. In brief, they were largely unsuccessful until the surrender of state-controlled administered pricing (through reimbursement rates) to managed care. Other than the United States, most governments have chosen to control prices or place limits on spending or availability of products and services (see examples in Chapter 1). These efforts at efficiency were made on behalf of maintaining affordable access to the system.

Invariably, many nations felt obligated to provide services that had been limited by their public budgets. This meant the use of private funds to meet the private demand for amounts and types of services that fell outside the public coffers. The private funds were aided by the use of quasi-public corporations or market-like incentives, as in the case of the British internal markets that created fundholders. In the United States, the effort has been to provide more equity in the provision of health care services. The issues of the medically uninsured or underinsured and the affordability of health care have been at the center of this effort. We will review some of the several mixes of private and public sharing of the provision of health care services later in this chapter.

Efficacy is the measure of the ability of a health care system to produce the desired results. This measure is subjectively evaluated depending upon the desired results. Do we want medical care on demand? Do market systems deliver more of the services we want at the time we want them? Do we expect a health care system to provide services to the public, regardless of the ability of consumers to pay for the services? Do we ration health care services of the basis of medical need? Is the distribution to be on the basis of who is first in the queue? Is distribution to be on the basis of the benefits received relative to the cost?

Private Goods, Public Goods, and Quasi-Public Goods

Private goods have two major characteristics. One is that those who are unable or unwilling to pay for a good or service are excluded from its benefits. A second characteristic is that "more for me means less for you." This implicitly assumes that the private good can be divided into discrete units. If I occupy the last available bed in a 200-bed private hospital, you are not able to find an available bed.

A *pure public good* is one for which nobody can be excluded from its benefits regardless of willingness or ability to pay. I may benefit from a publicly financed pollution control technology even if I object to the taxes imposed on the public to finance this program. A pure public good cannot be divided into discrete units; therefore, it cannot be sold to the public in the market. More pollution abatement for me will *not* mean less for you.

A *quasi-public good* appears when at least one of these two characteristics of public goods is not fully applicable at some stage of use. One example is that of a *price-excludable* public good. In 2005, the first $900 of a hospital stay is at the expense of the patient under Medicare coverage. Even though Medicare is publicly financed for people over the age of sixty-five in the United States, some low-income individuals who are unwilling or unable to pay the $900 will be *excluded* from the available hospital benefits under Medicare. A *congestible public good* prevents some people from acquiring a unit of a public good on the basis that more of the good for some has come at the expense of others. If a traffic snarl prevents the ambulance carrying me from arriving in time to be treated in the fully occupied emergency room, I will incur the costs of waiting or seeking alternative care.

When we place these definitions of private, public, and quasi-public goods in the context of equity and efficiency, we may become more aware of the implicit trade-offs. That is, as nations want to provide more access to health care they may incur greater costs in the form of inefficiency. Inadvertently, greater access may lead to limits on types and availability of services or rationing in the form of waiting for services. The capping of prices paid to suppliers may reduce the willingness of providers to continue production of their services and goods. When the U.S. Medicare system allowed its beneficiaries to take contracts with HMOs, the government negotiated a premium that attracted the HMOs, only to lower the premium later. Several HMOs opted to leave the Medicare system at that point. On the other hand, these issues are highly associated with publicly financed health care system. The trade-offs are significant. In the United States, greater efficiency is associated with market economies that have the primary financing of health care through private goods. However, this system has its major issues in the area of inadequate financial access to health care and health care insurance. The United States has recently readjusted its Medicare payments upward for beneficiaries having a higher illness experience.

The Basic Questions About Health Care Goods and Services

What to produce? How? How much? When? For whom? Who pays? These are the questions that are posed for all economies and that frame the choices for policy makers. The answers are conditioned on the presumptions underlying our political and economic frameworks. The history of any society reveals much about its philosophical direction as well as its predilection for free political and economic institutions.

What to Produce?

What to produce is predicated on a nation's willingness and ability to determine its "guns versus butter" menu. As demand increases for more health care services and particular products, who gets to decide which ones will eventually reach the consumers? A market-oriented economy that is competitively structured will allow consumers to vote with their effective demand for their preferences, constrained only by their incomes and the relative prices of the goods they seek. Under this competitive market structure, suppliers will respond to the preferences of consumers if the prices they are willing to pay equal or exceed the cost of the supplying firms. In the United States, consumers have demanded more pharmaceutical drugs, and firms here and abroad (mostly here) have responded in full measure. We know that this demand has been aided and abetted by vigorous promotional schemes, including payments to physicians. As Chapter 3, on pharmaceutical drug pricing, will reveal, increasing amounts of research funding is flowing into the United States, where there is an absence of price controls and where the returns on investment in research and development in pharmaceutical drugs have been higher than elsewhere. Market mechanisms respond to demand.

As noted elsewhere in this book, in government-regulated economies, the public budgets place limits on the amounts, types, and availability of these drugs. The regulated economies answer the *what* question in an environment of public budget–directed priorities. What to produce under these conditions becomes the "formulary quandary." Once a public budget appears, some official entity gets to decide which drugs make the acceptable list as a prerequisite for government funding.

How?

How to produce health care services and goods is, at first approximation, an engineering decision. However, in a market economy, the engineers do not always make the decision. The market mechanisms, under competitive conditions, demand that the goods or services be produced at the least cost combination of resources (land, labor, capital). Later in this book, the role of managed care in creating negotiated markets for health care services demonstrates the effects of markets on how to produce a hospital stay. The number of same-day surgeries, intensity of services in shorter hospital stays, and other outpatient services will have an impact on the number of admissions and the length of stay of patients in hospitals. In government-regulated systems, much of the production decision is based on predetermined technological considerations. The *how-to-produce* question is now having an interesting response in terms of management of diseases and evidence-based care. Rather than using a "reactive" response to illness, the new creed supports a "proactive" direction that tailors remedies and interventions to specific disease categories. Of course, this has interesting implications for health insurance. There is concern that insurance has played too large a role in the *what, how, how much, when,* and *for whom* questions. Some feel that insurance should stay with its original mission of financing health care through actuarial risk.

How Much?

We now address the question of *how much to produce* of health care goods and services in relationship to their costs and benefits. The other dimension is how much health care to extend at the margin of decision making. That is, should the patient have an additional two days in the hospital? Can we substitute a one-day surgery for a five-day hospital stay? Who decides? With respect to the first dimension, we may want to question whether more health care is necessarily better than less care. Some medical studies suggest that a higher supply of neonatologists and neonatal intensive care beds in an area that attracts patients to these services does little, if anything, to improve infant mortality rates over the rates in the less supplied areas (Kolata 2002, on-line pages). If we disaggregate the data, we find that a greater number of physicians typically results in a greater number of patient visits to doctors. However, we find no significant improvements in health measured in terms of rates of morbidity and mortality. Conversely, there is some evidence that decreases in the number of neonatologists below a national average number may increase the mortality rate per 10,000 births (Kolata 2002, on-line pages). Other studies have shown that benefits of health care discounted to a percent value and adjusted for inflation justify the rising costs of health care. Economists David Cutler and Mark McClellan found that lower "infant mortality and better treatment of heart attacks have been sufficiently great that they alone are about equal to the entire cost increase for medical care over time" ("Rising Medical Costs" 2001, *Wall Street Journal* on-line pages). Not all types of health care intervention justify care on the basis of benefit–cost analysis. A significant study in 1995 entitled "Five Hundred Life-Saving Interventions and Their Cost-Effectiveness" (Tengs, et al. 1995, pp. 370–380) found that there are great variations in morbidity and mortality outcomes in different diagnostic and treatment categories.

The market and its price mechanisms exert rigorous standards on the amount of medical care delivered in response to the amount demanded. Providers of care are restrained by costs. Since a high proportion of employees' health insurance costs are paid by their employers' health plans, these employers have considerable weight in negotiating the premiums and benefit coverage with preferred provider organizations (PPOs). The costs of health care coverage are considerable for the auto makers. General Motors reports health care costs of $1,525 per vehicle in 2004. General Motors, Ford Motor Company, and Daimler Chrysler pressured their PPO, Blues Preferred Plus, to reduce the number of medical doctors and to reduce the payments to the M.D.s staying in the plan. In good old-fashioned bargaining style, the physicians returned the favor by taking the PPO to court (Hawkins 2005). This is a witness to private market forces that are able to respond to an increase in demand for health care services and insurance coverage. Americans want more health care and they get more health care since they are willing and able to pay for it. This is part of the efficiency of a market system. If the prices move consumers and their employers beyond their budget constraints, pressure is exerted to reduce the underlying costs, as in the previous example. This kind of a market response does not account for the equity concerns of access to the system by low-income and uninsured individuals and households. Also, as costs of health care increase, there is an inevitable desire to economize on the expense and, perhaps, some of the less vital services. As out-of-pocket expenses rise, consumers usually begin to substitute less expensive and alternative health care goods and services. We begin to see the possibilities of these forms of economizing with the introduction of health savings accounts as discussed in Chapter 6.

In contrast, the *how much* question is usually answered differently and in a more explicitly rationed manner by government-regulated or nationalized systems. There are examples in Chapter 1 about the rationing of kidney dialysis under the National Health Service in the United Kingdom. When health care costs increase beyond the public budget, the typical responses in these regulated schemes is to limit types, quantities, and availability of the products and services. This may result in denial of services or a long queue. The *how much* is also a function of supply. There is no mystery attached to pharmaceutical research and development (R&D) funds moving from other countries to the United States in recent years. Without government controls on the pricing of pharmaceutical drugs and the increase in the number of new branded items, the returns to innovation and marketing costs have been very attractive. The pharmaceutical companies claim a need for these returns to capture high fixed costs and to provide a basis for future research.

Most other countries, as discussed later in this book, have some form of direct or indirect price controls and formularies that dictate the drugs to be publicly subsidized. The general question of how much to produce is illustrated and explained in Chapter 1. The inverse relationship between the percentage of a nation's GDP devoted to health care expenditures and the percentage of health care expenditures that are publicly funded suggests that the public budgets act as effective constraints on spending for health care. The United States has the lowest percentage of publicly provided funding but the highest percentage of GDP for health care expenditures (see Table 1.1, page 8, for comparison nations). The private demand for health care services has a more reflective response in terms of quantity, type, and availability than is apparent in the regulated or nationalized system. A contributing factor in the United States is the greater level of consumer income. Since health care is a normal good, we would expect at least a proportional increase in demand for health care goods and services with a given increase in income.

When?

When to produce health care services is a supplier/government decision that is influenced by the responses to other questions. For example, some health care services are rationed in the form of postponing the delivery of care until a later date. There are queues for some forms of elective surgery in Canada. A patient can receive the benefits of a pharmaceutical drug only after it is placed on the formulary. In the United States, Medicaid services become available when consumers meet the thresholds of income and assets. This is also an issue of resource allocation. Should policy makers place a higher priority on the care and financing of the elderly, who have relatively short life spans? Should we, instead, devote more of our resources to disease categories that have a longer period of returns on costs? People with AIDS or the HIV virus among the younger age groups, including children, will have long pay-off periods to recoup the private and social costs of care.

Consumers in market-directed economies make implicit or explicit decisions on choices between consumption and savings. Consumers have different preferences for current consumption and future consumption. A dollar saved today means one less dollar to spend today. However, a dollar saved today may mean more than a dollar available for future consumption. The difference would depend on the rates of inflation over time, the interest rate on saved dollars, and the rate of taxation on interest income. The government role can influence these saving and consumption decisions. So, if competitive market forces are in place, changes in the tax code can have an influence. The health savings accounts (HSAs) under the Medicare reform of 2003 provide an example of how government can influence the incentives to save. Since the HSAs are heavily tax advantaged, there is an incentive to save for future medical expenses. If successful, these accounts would mean that there would be fewer out-of-pocket costs for future health care services and their benefits. Conversely, if current health care services are heavily subsidized by government and insurance coverage, consumers might spend more and seek more care in the present. Thus, when to produce health care services can be influenced by market initiatives as well as by government policies.

For Whom?

For whom to produce the health care services is, in many ways, a composite of the other four questions discussed earlier. Specifically, policy, demographic factors, and socioeconomic status are determining factors in the distribution of health care services. The answers to this question have been framed by the defining characteristics of private, quasi-public, and public goods. Policy parameters are formed by the relative weights put on equity versus efficiency concerns. The trade-offs develop as emphasis on access and fair distribution of health care services comes at the expense of less efficient use of our scarce health care resources. Conversely, as market incentives direct more attraction to efficiency, there may be inadvertent loss of access to the system for people without health insurance or adequate income.

When it is clear that a government chooses to regulate health care through public regulation, the market "terms of exchange" will be affected. That is, the prices, types, quantities, and availability of health care goods and services will be adversely affected. Under these circumstances, governments must either say we have exhausted our public resources for health care or that we need to ration care in some manner. For example, we may ration kidney dialysis so that care can go to the most needy or so that we can direct resources to other health care priorities. Alternatively, governments may wish to seek private funds to fill any gaps in care. Some governments may wish to create a quasi-public authority or agency to provide care with public oversight and some financing support. In the United States, the presumption is that the allocation of relatively scarce health care resources is largely based on demand for health care goods and services. The market may need to be more competitive; the government can respond with use of anti-trust action. The government can also use its taxing and spending power to assist the market. Revision in the tax codes made health savings accounts attractive to consumers and investors. HSAs are heavily tax advantaged. Under Medicare reform in 2003, private insurance companies are required to be in competitive markets in order to offer policies for the pharmaceutical drug coverage. The hope is that the private insurance markets will be better risk assumers and empower Medicare recipients to find lower prices for their brand-name drugs. The government provides coverage to consumers for major portions of their costs. The Medicare Modernization Act (2003) has a number of programs that allow low-income individuals to obtain significantly reduced prices for their coverage. Thus, government policies will affect the *for whom* question by regulation, subsidizing, taxing, or rationing health care services.

The *for whom* question is also somewhat dependent on demographic factors. As the population ages in the United States, more of our health care resources are directed to older Americans. Each older American now has more health care technologies, services, and products (especially pharmaceutical) available than ever before. If these new products are purchased, even at constant prices, health care expenditures for the elderly increase. If there are more people in the over-sixty-five age cohort and if each senior citizen uses more services more regularly, the increase in the quantity (Q) factor of the price (P) times (Q) equation ($P \times Q = TE$) results in a real increase in total health care expenditures (TE). If the prices of new products and services are higher than the old products (adjusted for inflation), we witness a major increase in resources used for the elderly. Similarly, with substantial differences in the need for health care for infants through teenagers as compared to other age groups, population and birth increases would imply that the *for whom* question would favor the very young. Recently there has been a spate of interest and action in providing state and federal health insurance coverage for this age group. Also, we know that we spend disproportionately high amounts of our resources on the final days of care for the elderly, at least in the United States.

Socioeconomic factors, particularly for low-income households and single female–headed households, lead to public support programs for health care. Federal, state, and local budgets are being overwhelmed by expenditures for Medicaid, the public health insurance program for low-income people. We also know that many of the preventative measures used by other income groups are not as readily available for low-income households. Therefore, those households suffer the "diseases of the poor" that require relatively high amounts of public assistance. The *for whom* question is answered by social recognition of need.

Who Pays?

If the policy extremes of nationalized universal affordable care for all and the free market with no government involvement are rejected as not being practical or viable, we are left with various public and private "mix and match" systems as public policy choices. To illustrate these choices, this last section of this chapter will give examples of how these mixed systems have fared. We will complete this chapter with a policy perspective on public-private systems. We should be reminded that there are many variations of private and public financing. Government can provide health care as a public good but elect to have the care produced privately. We have many examples of this in the United States, including Medicare and Medicaid programs, national defense contracts, and public highways. Some governments provide for prisons but decide to have the prisons operate as privately run firms, presumably on the basis of greater cost-effectiveness.

One of the difficulties, other than simple bureaucracy, is the establishment of prices that reflect the value of the services rendered in a government-administered program. Who pays depends, in large measure, on what one expects to get in value. If the government commands the location and types of distribution, we may find that the distribution of health services is not compatible with the relative need and preferences of consumers (taxpayers). The result can adversely affect the ability of the system to function as well as it would in competitive market settings. Some in the U.K. would model a reformed National Health Service (NHS) with removal or reduction of a command post or centrally administered design "within the framework of a publicly funded, free-at-the-point-of-delivery service" (Smith 2000, p. 6). This proposal would give greater authority to the NHS Trusts to base priorities on need and to pay employees based on their contributions. Consideration would be given to changing the operation of the NHS Trusts to that of not-for-profit-organizations in a quest for more efficiency. The bottom line of this reform would require that "patients should have a price on their heads, and GPs should compete to retain or attract them. The more explicit the fee, the more new GP practices would be encouraged to move into the market and compete aggressively for patients" (Smith 2000, p. 6).

Who pays invariably involves a combination of contributions from insurance, government (taxpayers), employers, and "out-of-pocket" consumer sources. Does an insurance company or another third party pay in accordance with the market values? Is there a payment consistent with the benefits of the services? Later in this book, *disease management* is identified as a countervailing method of both controlling costs and being a proactive rather than a reactive strategy for the provision of health care services. Even effective reactive systems often fall short of the more comprehensive, yet disease-specific, team program characteristic of disease management. These programs identify chronic illnesses such as diabetes, congestive heart failure, asthma, and depression, which comprise almost two-thirds of rising health care costs (Andrews 2003, p. BU9). The question raised here is *who pays?* In the case of the Hill Physicians Medical Group in San Ramon, California, the programs of disease management are being sponsored by the physician group through a bonus incentive plan. This plan will pay a physician an annual bonus of approximately 10 percent for successfully monitoring the outcomes of patients including decreases in visits to the emergency room, cholesterol levels, and weight levels. This control of the regimen of the patients is enhanced by daily communications and a schedule for regular visits to the physician. This is *not* a program that is directed by insurance companies or employers. Indeed, some patients in disease management programs are denied reimbursement by insurance companies. The "old" system often paid for the care only if patients were hospitalized or had sought care in emergency rooms (Andrews 2003, p. BU9). The old system reacted to disease outcomes while the new system attempts to manage diseases to reduce or prevent negative outcomes. Who pays depends more on reimbursement systems than it does on a performance basis.

Who pays for health care services is often based on who assumes the responsibility for the financing of health care. Clearly, payment for health care services has become a mixed private-public function. In the United States, large businesses finance major portions of their employees' health care. This becomes problematic as the costs of health care services continue to rise, particularly in the United States. Health care benefits for retired workers have traditionally been covered by their former employers. The disproportionate rise in the over-sixty-five age cohort and the increase in new medical technology, products, and services have combined to place additional burdens on employers who help finance benefits for their retired workers. While 97 percent of employers provide coverage for health care, only 36 percent of the large companies in the United States in 2003 still provided retiree coverage at least up to eligibility for Medicare (Gross 2004, p. BU6). In 2004, the Medicare program in the United States began to cover some prescription drug costs for its beneficiaries (those over sixty-five years old). In effect this shifted some of the costs of health care from employers to taxpayers (see Chapter 7, on Medicare reform). Who pays depends on the mix of public and private shares of the costs of health care. The health savings accounts created for first use in 2004 attempt to reduce the payments for health care for consumers and for society by offering tax-advantaged savings.

This program could have long-term effects of shifting responsibility for decisions to consumers and their physicians and relegating the financing function to insurance firms. Who pays is directly affected by public and private shares. Since only fourteen of every one hundred dollars spent on health care in 2003 came directly as out-of-pocket expense, and since our payment system is heavily subsidized by insurance, employees, and government, there has been an obscuring of the question of who pays. This system has led to "obvious inefficiencies, such as consumer insensitivity to medical prices and a tendency to overuse 'free' health care" (Pollock 2003a, p. A14).

The *who pays* question is sometimes answered by risk adjustment. With the increasing use of private insurance for the U.S. Medicare population, risk adjustment is necessary for the success of any programs that use market incentives. It would be normal to expect private insurance companies to take on the lowest risk consumers. In 2004, the revised Medicare program, which includes some coverage for pharmaceutical drugs and uses private insurance firms, made 30 percent of the payments risk adjusted. The risk adjustment will increase until all payments will be subjected to risk adjustment (Landers 2003, on-line pages). This type of adjustment is critical to the understanding on any mixed system. Government is not in the risk business and needs to convey the tasks of risk adjustment to the appropriate financial and insurance institutions. In this case, the government provides health insurance but private firms produce the insurance. These firms need to be directed to adjust the risks in accord with public policy. In the absence of a government directive, market failure is likely, as evidenced in the former Medicare + Choice program, which attracted the healthier beneficiaries and caused the government a deficit of over 3 billion dollars each year. The replacement program, Medicare Advantage, pays a greater premium to private firms for beneficiaries with more past health problems (Landers 2003b, on-line pages). For this public-private mix to work, the private firm needs to be paid its costs based, in part, by actuarial estimates. Otherwise, the firm will pull out, as many did under the former Medicare + Choice program. On the other hand, the government does not want to pay a rent to the private firm that might want to reduce its risk by picking only the healthiest subscribers. We will see if Medicare gets it right!

Public financing of medical care necessitates budgets that often are extended to provide medical services under conditions of rising costs and growing numbers of low-income families. The resultant deficits have created the political need to reduce spending and/or place limits on the number of eligible recipients. In California, Governor Arnold Schwarzenegger proposed lowering costs in the health programs including Medi-Cal (California's Medicaid) and in the Healthy Families state-federal insurance program for the near poor. The Healthy Families program would place a limit based on current enrollment that would deny care to approximately 300,000 eligible children (Broder 2004, on-line pages). With constraints on public spending for health care, the consequence or trade-off is often measured in terms of a limit on quantity, availability, or type of service. Private budgets or public-private ventures appear to be more responsive to the needs and wants of consumers. Thus, the *who pays* question has somewhat of an indeterminant answer. In effect, when government "pays" for health care, current or future taxpayers are the contributors. We could, to some degree, say that past taxpayers may have contributed to any surplus used to finance current government programs. The difference between taxpayers footing the bill and consumers paying directly out of pocket with aid from insurance is significant. As with one of the major themes of this book, consumers get to pick their menu of health care services based on their preferences and willingness to pay. When public budgets prevail, taxpayers pay for an administered menu that is limited and restricted.

In light of this dichotomy of public and private spending effects, some public authorities have decided to transfer part of the responsibility of providing and financing health care to semi-independent or public benefit corporations. In the state of New York, Nassau and Westchester counties have provided examples of these operations in the form of the Nassau Health Care Corporation and the Westchester Health Care Corporation. The major constituent hospitals are the Nassau University Medical Center and the Westchester Medical Center. The basis for the change was to reduce overbearing government bureaucracy and to increase the impetus to seek more efficient methods of operation. However, the change from a fully government-based operation to a fully competitive market system has not been realized. There are benefits associated with the change, such as greater roles in labor dismissals and, in general, greater discretion in business decisions. Still, county officials make appointments and the counties provide subsidies and fiscal support for the issuance for bonds (Lambert and Healy 2004, on-line pages). The answer to the *who pays* question is somewhat more determinate in favor of market-directed decisions, which should give greater authority to the consumer, even in an asymmetrical health care market with an imbalance of information on the side of medical providers.

Much of the "who pays" question is answered by the relative use of market competition. A major debate issue in the United States has been the role of private insurance in the revised Medicare program enacted in December 2003 to gradually provide pharmaceutical drug coverage for those over the age of sixty-five. In brief, most seniors will need to secure their insurance coverage from private insurers. Since these drugs are *not* the subject of price controls, there is a perceived need to assure competition in insurance markets. Prices *should* be disciplined by the competition. Therefore, the consumer can benefit by choosing the low-cost retailer or insurance company. In theory, the consumer would pay less and have more choices than in a government system with controls on prices and a formulary that restricts the type and quantity of drugs available. This new program of Medicare is discussed more completely in Chapter 7. There is the hope that the infusion of market forces will enable Americans to pay less than the current rise of approximately 250 billion dollars a year (McGinley and Lueck 2003, on-line pages). This scenario is similar to the choices the Canadians face in the battle between government advocates who want to increase spending for health care and those who want the private sector to be more responsive to health care needs. This happens as many of the provinces are limiting the services covered by publicly financed insurance. There has been an increase in physical examinations and magnetic resonance imagery (MRI). Who pays? Those who are able to use private services for access will pay. Those who cannot pay privately will have to accept the limited public menus ("Fistfuls of Health Dollars" 2004, pp. 33–34).

The public-private mix of services also involves the question of private access to services not funded by government. Should a private citizen be permitted to enter into private contracts for the provision of these services? Should the citizen be allowed to buy services prohibited as unreasonable or too experimental by Medicare? How about private contracts for Medicare beneficiaries who want additional amounts of services beyond what Medicare covers? In all of those situations, we assume that private contracts would be paid for services *not* already billed to Medicare. The answer to all of these questions was, initially, "no" during the earlier part of the Clinton administration. However, subsequent court actions and reviews by the federal administration produced a finding that there was no prohibition against these private contracts. Consequently, markets began to develop in which consumers could pay privately for new medical devices *before* probable approval by Medicare. *Who pays* also becomes *can we pay?* ("A Victory for Private Medicine" 1999, p. A26).

Through the use of buyers' clubs and web sites offering discounted and negotiated prices, consumers are able to get more medical services at lower costs. These arrangements are particularly attractive for employers, who require more and more of their health coverage costs to be shared by employees, as well as for the uninsured and users of noninsured alternative medical treatments (Freudenheim 2000, pp. A1 and C19).

We conclude this chapter with economic analysis from two studies on the effects of public funding of health care services on outcomes. A study by Mark C. Berger and Jodi Messer (2002, p. 2105[9]), using 1960–1992 data from twenty OECD countries is central to the focus on the need to reform health care systems. Since most reform efforts have involved the shares of private and public funding relative to the percentage of GDP devoted to health care spending, this study considers health outcomes in the context of variations, across nations, such as demographic factors and socioeconomic, educational, and income levels. Public shares of health care financing have increased for many countries in recent years except in the United Kingdom and Germany, where there have been some decreases. The findings of Berger and Messer's study are that:

1. Increases in the share of public funding are associated with higher mortality rates.
2. Increases in the share of public funding may result in a "less productive mix of services or less efficient provision of services" (2002, p. 2105[9]).
3. Improved health outcomes, including mortality rates, are associated with increases in ambulatory coverage relative to increases in in-patient coverage.
4. The policy implication offered in this study is clearly stated: "As countries increase the level of their health expenditures, they may want to avoid increasing the proportion of their expenditures that are publicly financed" (2002, p. 2105[9]).

These findings are not unexpected in view of the trade-offs of regulated and publicly financed systems referenced in these first two chapters.

The limitations on necessary drug therapy for breast cancer patients in countries with public budget constraints has led to much lower survival rates than in the United States, where the use of the drug is primarily financed through private insurance. This example and others are used throughout this book to illustrate the trade-offs inherent in public financing of health care.

Another study of mixed public and private financing by Stephen Globerman and Adrian Vining (1998, pp. 57–80) provides another policy perspective on the mix of private and public financing of health care. The study analyzed the possible effects of private financing on the level of public budget for health care. The authors also investigate the claim that private financing will contribute to increased health care costs and, hence, decrease the real value of public health care expenditures. Results of the study appear to contradict these suggestions. Rather, "they provide support for the view that attempts to restrict the availability of private financing will erode support for a public plan that is operating with excess demand" (p. 77). There are the associated trade-offs of limits or reductions in public budgets in the form of less availability of health care services. Globerman and Vining counter the argument that high shares of private financing of health care relative to public shares produce higher cost increases for health care. They cite the situation in the United States where the introduction of Medicare and Medicaid caused inflation to accelerate. We could add the warning that the Medicare coverage of pharmaceutical drugs as an entitlement for seniors could increase health care costs dramatically. Globerman and Vining also feel that greater access and technological advances in the United States may really be understated as quality improvements. In general, the results of this study "argue in favor of allowing more privately financed health care, on the margin, as an important supplement to public provision" (p. 78). We need to keep this perspective in mind as we examine a number of health care issues in this book, beginning with pharmaceutical drug pricing and availability in the next chapter.

3

The Pricing of Drugs

Who Benefits and Who Pays?

The Setting and the Questions

The oft-cited saying, "You only get what you pay for" (father-in-law Arch Gifford, circa 1980) might be challenged by "Do you want to pay for what you get?" Thus, the pricing of drugs is part of the social dichotomy of entitlement versus individual responsibilities. If I am old or poor, should others pay for my health care needs? If I am wealthy and in need of a prescription drug that will improve my life, should I pay for these benefits? These are normative propositions that get into the "could have," "should have," and "ought to have" value-laden issues. These issues relate to moral, philosophical, and ideological beliefs. Economists are prepared to dismiss these value sets in favor of pure or positive economic analysis. This analysis centers on factors that explain price and other economic changes, the understanding of "what is." Alternatively, we can accept one of the normative propositions that suggests senior citizens should have some, if not all, of their prescription drugs expenditures paid by others. Economists can say, "You can go that way but it will cost society a lot!" In other words, it might not be the most cost-effective way to achieve the social objective. Are the gains to society greater than the costs to society? If so, there is a welfare gain. If not, there is a welfare loss. The greater good for the greater number (welfare gain) is the axiom for positive economic analysis. How can positive economic analysis guide government health care policy on the pricing of drugs? Can the microeconomic role of allocating relatively scarce health care resources to their most efficient (production) and most desired (consumption) uses be compatible with government's desire to finance drug consumption redistributively? Can we say that the presumption in America is that of limited government as championed by Thomas

Jefferson? If so, we would want to put the free market as its economic agent. Do market prices tell us anything about consumer preferences? Are these prices telling us anything about the relative scarcity of drug resources? Do these prices tell us anything about the willingness of pharmaceutical companies to undertake risks commensurate with a fair rate of return or profit? Do market prices for drugs tell us anything about the shares of world drug production by a nation without price controls? Or are these prices simply the outcome of monopolistic control, that is, rents extracted from consumers and society? Would price controls result in significantly lower innovation and research in the production of new pharmaceutical products? How do we measure the benefits, private and social, of pharmaceutical products? In order to get at some answers to these questions, we will look first at the role of prices in competitive markets. Then, we will be able to analyze the combined effects of market, institutional, and government adjustments to the competitive model in the real world of pharmaceutical prices.

The Role of Prices in a Competitive Economy

We will assume a competitive market structure for the buying and selling of pharmaceutical products in the United States. We do this to uncover the role and functions of prices in a market-oriented economy. Later we will recognize the effects of government, institutional, and market imperfections on pharmaceutical products.

There are three functions of prices: signals, disciplinarians, and rationers. As signals, prices reflect consumer choices and preferences. What goods are consumers willing and able to buy? Think of a set of traffic lights. If the providers get a green light, consumers are saying the price is right according to our incomes and preferences. An amber light suggests that consumers are considering substitutes. Perhaps their preference for the good or service is waning given its price relative to other goods and consumer income. A red light directs producers to design and provide different products and services. The reduced demand is no longer sufficient to pay for producers' costs, including a fair return or profit.

As disciplinarians, prices "regulate" the competitive behavior of producers or providers. Consumers, through prices, tell providers that they need to provide a better product or a lower price on the current product. Otherwise, consumers will "vote" with their dollars by buying from competitive suppliers. This action requires consumer sovereignty and choices.

As rationers, prices put pressure on consumers and suppliers to economize on scarce resources. Relatively scarce resources carry high price tags. We expect providers to use relatively few scarce (high-price) resources or to "economize" on these resources (land, labor, capital, entrepreneurial). Conversely, the relatively abundant resources would carry lower price tags and be used more. As the scarce resources are used more sparingly, their prices would decrease; as the more abundant resources are used more freely, their prices would increase. So the price mechanism encourages the saving or economizing of scarce resources. This releases resources for the production of more goods and services. This rationing process is either explicit or implicit in all health care and pharmaceutical markets. It holds for nations that primarily use markets or for nations that have nationalized health care or insurance. There will be more about rationing later in this chapter.

There are certain requirements or assumptions that need to be in place in order for these price functions to be operative. Prices operate in the context of capitalism. This system requires the following:

1. Ownership and protection of *private property* as the *basis* of the system. Private ownership is the antithesis of socialism and communism.
2. A *competitive market.* Competition is the *whip* of the system. This means that firms are *price takers.* Firms must charge the going or competitive price, or suffer losses, or exit from the market. There are no price makers in a competitive market.
3. The expectation of *profits.*
4. Free *mobility* of resources (particularly for labor and capital and entrepreneurial ability).
5. *Consumer sovereignty.* The *consumer directs* the action in the market. As indicated earlier, the consumer signals the producers to indicate whether the price is in accord with the consumer's willingness and ability to pay it.
6. *Distribution* by *contribution* (productivity). Those who provide the most for the economy get the most out of the economy at the margin of their contribution. Those who work harder, invest more in their human resources including education, assume risks, make innovations, and increase productivity receive more of the accumulation of income and goods than those who contribute less. This connection between production and the rewards of income

and goods provides the incentive to make long-term improvements to our well-being as a nation.

In the earlier days of fee-for-service health care, "the expenditures
incurred in the medical system were largely taken as a given by all insurers. The net result was that private insurers acted as both price and
quantity takers in the market for health services" (Newhouse 2002, p.
10). This means that insurers played the role of financing health care
after the prices and quantities for health care were determined in the
market. Today, managed care organizations are major players in determining the pricing and quantity of health care for consumers.

The expected outcomes of competitive market forces include efficiency (see definition in Chapter 2), a match of prices consumers are
willing to pay and prices suppliers are willing to accept, and mutually
acceptable exchange. This exchange between buyer and seller benefits
at least one of the parties, if not both, and neither party is worse off than
before the exchange. These market exchanges allow for more choices
for consumers. Implicit in all of this is that the market encourages continuing exchanges and growth in the economy. In addition to these applied microeconomic issues, we also need to consider the effects of
increased government funding in an era of budget constraints. We will
examine these macro issues under policy implications in the last chapter. To put the above theory in the context of pharmaceutical products, a
consumer would pay only for the extra or marginal cost (MC) for Pfizer's
production and distribution of its top-selling, cholesterol-lowering
Lipitor, which would be significantly less than its U.S. price. The U.S.
price includes a return on its fixed costs of innovation and research.
Theoretically, as long as Pfizer receives marginal revenue greater than
its marginal cost, its profits increase. The addition to total cost, marginal
cost, would be less than the addition to total revenue, marginal revenue.
Thus, Pfizer would continue to produce Lipitor until its marginal cost
was equal to the marginal revenue associated with the last unit produced;
its profits would be maximized. As indicated earlier, this pricing would
not provide the incentive to develop new products since investors would
be disappointed with an inadequate return on capital investments. Investors, including the pharmaceutical companies, would look elsewhere to
find higher returns given a similar level of risk. The competitive model
has this virtue of the consumer getting goods at "cost" (price = minimum average cost = marginal cost). However, the producer or investor

lacks the financial ability to reinvest profits and the incentive to do so with only "normal" profits. These profits are only sufficient to maintain the state-of-the art technology. This represents the dilemma of anti-trust courts: the enormous benefits of advances in technology through economies of scale versus the need to keep competition viable to ensure fair prices for consumers. Do producers need greater profits in order to innovate and do research for improved and needed drugs?

Who pays and who benefits? Economists can approach this problem by accepting the premise or normative judgment that "we *should* have increased drug availability for senior citizens." Then the question would become "what is the most cost-effective way to provide this coverage without intruding on the substance of the system of savings accounts?" (See HSAs or MSAs, Chapter 6.) Over time, seniors would be using some of their savings to receive *their* benefits from the use of prescription drugs. If we are concerned about who pays, we would require greater contributions from the wealthiest and lesser contributions from the lowest-income population, with zero contributions from those with no income.

The government has other tools, including regulations and anti-trust litigations, to influence economic outcomes. There are a number of institutional practices, including tier pricing, pharmaceutical benefit managers, brand name pricing, price discrimination, monopoly pricing, and generic competition, that also affect the availability and distribution of drugs. Institutions and firms are vying for controlling roles in the pricing and distribution of pharmaceutical products.

It is both popular and political to promote the government as the responsible agent for the provision, if not the production, of nonabusive drugs for consumers. As a corollary, the government becomes the single buyer, single payer, and rationer, a.k.a. distributor, of pharmaceutical products. This role would likely entail control of prices and quantity of drugs for different consumer groups. In contrast, the less popular and more empirically effective method would be the use of price and market mechanisms. This method would ferret out the most economical uses of our resources to satisfy consumer preferences. It would allow the "*scientific* advances in pharmaceutical research and bio-technology and *institutional* advances in drug testing, information processing, and the dissemination of knowledge among scientists, manufacturers, doctors, patients, consumers and managed care organizations" (Calfee 2000, pp. 1–3, emphasis is that of the author, John E. Calfee).

In order to better ascertain the role of markets in the determination of prices and quantities available of drugs, we will digress to identify various types of markets. A market is defined as the meeting place for buyers and sellers. It is where exchanges occur. We have labor markets, capital markets, commodity markets, futures markets, money markets, and product markets. These market "places" need not occupy a physical space. It is wherever transactors make exchanges; it can be E-bay or another electronic site. Indeed, some Americans are buying on-line drugs from Canadian pharmacies. The market can have peculiar institutional features, as certainly is the case for pharmaceutical products. The particular arrangements for producers, wholesalers, retailers, and other intermediaries can have profound effects on the outcomes of markets. That is, the market features will be reflected in the prices, quantities, availability, and access of product for the consumer. The ways in which consumers and sellers organize themselves are significant. The next section identifies types of markets.

Types of Markets

1. *Free Competitive Markets.* These are markets in which there are so many buyers and sellers (transactors) that no single transactor or group of transactors can determine the terms of exchange (price, quality, and quantity available). The prices will be determined solely by the exchanges in the markets of all buyers and sellers. Each firm will have to price its goods and services at the "going price," that is, the market price. This means that each firm is a "price taker" rather than a "price maker." Assuming a perfectly competitive market, each firm's price is equal to its minimum average cost of production as well as its marginal cost of producing an extra unit. The buyers are able to coax the producer to supply another pair of shoes or another dosage of a prescription drug at exactly the marginal cost of production. These costs include an implicit cost if the rate of return from an alternate use of one's resources (land, capital, labor, entrepreneurial ability) is greater than the firm is receiving on its current use of resources. This assumes that the alternatives are at the same risk level. A mom and a pop in a small business may work in excess of fourteen hours a day. If they were to spend those hours in alternative employment, their income from work could increase. So, it costs them to work in their own business. Even though none of us will ever witness a perfectly competitive market, we can appreciate a system that encourages each firm to be cost-effective so as to stay in business. If

one firm does not produce and sell at the competitive price, some other firm will do it. Imagine that Wal-Mart would be allowed to force producers of prescription drugs to reduce prices to that same low level of disposable diapers. "Wal-Martizing" has become synonymous with the ability of a retailer to extract major discounts from producers and wholesalers. These kinds of competitive pressures have been largely responsible for very low rates of inflation in the United States and, more importantly, lower prices on many consumer goods for low-income families. So competitive markets make better use of the nation's resources and allow consumers to enjoy a plethora of choices of goods at low prices. If we economize on the use of scarce resources, we will be able to have more public and private goods and services than would have been otherwise possible.

2. *Imperfect Competition.* In the real world, perfectly competitive markets do not exist. There are imperfections in product markets, labor markets, and capital markets. The imperfections can stem from the behavior of the transactors (buyers and sellers), the institutions, and the government. Pharmaceutical companies can engage in monopoly prices aided by patent protection. They can also practice price discrimination by charging higher prices to customers with higher incomes. Consumers can form buyer groups. The government can help finance drug purchases through insurance programs. These and other imperfections and interferences with market pricing will be discussed later in this chapter.

3. *Government-regulated Markets.* These markets are more common outside the United States. They feature direct price controls on drugs. Canada has direct price controls and also provides national insurance through its provinces. Government can exercise control of quantities of imports and exports. We will examine these and other government influences later.

4. *Negotiated Markets.* These are markets in which the government sanctions the setting of prices and availability of services or goods by group representatives of buyers and sellers. Managed care organizations are brokers between groups of employers (buyers for employees) and groups of providers (sellers: hospitals, physicians). This arrangement is somewhat akin to collective bargaining between labor unions and employers. Even though there is a market exchange, it is not of buyers and sellers acting as individuals. Rather, it is groups negotiating quantity availability and price. The net result is a price determined in advance of the actual buyer–seller exchange.

5. *Brokered or Individual (No Insurance) Markets.* In these markets, either or both of the participants may benefit from "stepping outside the system" and arranging a mutually satisfactory price and quantity/quality for the service rendered. The server may feel that a lower-than-normal price is preferred to a normal price contingent upon the filing or completing of complex, time-consuming, and costly paperwork. The buyer may feel that the lower price with no insurance premiums to pay is preferable to a higher price plus insurance premiums, which may not reflect his actuarial risk or preference for insurance.

6. *Administered Pricing.* In these markets, the price is established by the seller either by government edict or by monopolistic control of markets. This market can be a variation of imperfectly competitive markets or government-regulated markets as described earlier.

We will place all of this analysis in the context of "The Problem" of pharmaceutical pricing in the next section.

The Problem

The most explicit problem for pharmaceuticals is that of price increases. Implicit in this problem are the trade-offs that we will discuss later in this chapter. These trade-offs include issues of access, distribution, and availability of drugs for consumers as well as issues of risks, a high fixed costs to variable costs ratio, and incentives to innovate and do research on the suppliers side. Also, since prescription drugs are a major factor in increasing U.S. health care expenditures, they have become a political issue, particularly for Medicare reform. Americans are the largest consumers of pharmaceutical products in the world. U.S. pharmaceutical firms produce more of the brand-name entities than any other nation. And the research and innovation for new drugs is increasingly occurring in the United States, which has the single highest share of profits.

Retail drug purchases in the United States increased at "an average annual rate of 15.6 percent between 2000 and 2002" (Smith 2004, p. 161). This is a product of the equation $P \times Q = TE$, or the prices of drugs × the quantity of drugs sold equals the total expenditures on drugs. Thus, price changes in drugs are not the only basis for changes in total drug spending. Even if drug prices were *not* to change from one year to the next, we still might expect increases in total spending or expenditures on drugs. The entry of managed care firms provided greater drug coverage, which also increased the quantity of spending. There are many factors on the quantity-of-use side. We know that there is a disporportionate share of the population that is over sixty-five years of age. This share is being compounded by the "baby boomers" age cohort rapidly reaching sixty-five years of age and beyond. This age group is the largest consumer of drugs (33 percent) while representing only about 13 percent of the population ("Drug-Price Program Notes" 2000, p. A18). Thus, even with no drug price changes and no new drugs, the sheer increase in the number of consumers means health care expenditures would increase. If we add all of the new drugs together with their greater daily use, we see an even greater increase in the quantity of prescription drugs sold. If we also account for price increases for drugs, the drug spending increases are accentuated. There are upward biases in the way generics and new medical entities or drugs are calculated for the index of price changes. We will discuss these biases, especially for generic substitutes, later in this chapter. Using intensity of use as one factor and drug prices as another factor to account for growth in U.S. prescription drug spending from 1980 to 2002, we note the changes in relative effect of these two factors. "Much of the rise in spending over the past decade has been attributed to steady growth in use, which incorporates a shift to consumers to newer drugs at higher prices. A smaller portion has been accounted for by price increases among existing drugs" (Smith 2004, p. 161).

Prescription drug spending in the United States increased rapidly in the 1980s and 1990s. Part of this increase is explained by the larger increases in the drug price index than for the price index for all health care expenditures (Smith 2004, pp. 161–162). Government figures show the average annual percentage increase in constant 2001 dollars of prescription drugs to be fairly consistent from 1996–2001 at around 11.8 percent. The projection for the period 2001–2005 is an increase of 10 percent and an increase from 2005 to 2010 of only 6.6. percent (U.S. House, Ways and Means 2003). For international comparisons using U.S. dollars in terms of purchasing power parity (US & PPP) in 1998, the United States had a total expenditure per capita on pharmaceuticals of $442, which was the second highest amount next to France at $447. The United Kingdom was $229, Germany $300, and Canada $353 for the same year. In 1997–98, the U.S. expenditure on pharmaceuticals as a percentage of total health expenditures was 10.1. For France it was 21.9 percent, Germany 12.7 percent, Canada 15 percent, and the United Kingdom 16.3 percent (OECD 2001, p. 47). Please be advised that since total health care expenditures are absolutely lower in these countries compared to the United States, any significant pharmaceutical expenditures are going to be a relatively high percentage of total health expenditures.

In the United States, payment for drugs and the role of institutional forces further explain both constraining and contributing influences on prices and quantity of prescription drugs. In 2002, consumers paid 30 percent of their drug expenses out of pocket. This 30 percent out-of-pocket share in 2002 contrasts with 96 percent in 1960, 66 percent in 1980, and 50 percent in 1994 (Smith 2004, p. 163). Clearly, the lower the out-of-pocket share, the less constrained consumers are in terms of demand for the prescribed drugs. Other factors include managed care influences, pharmacy benefit managers who negotiate discounts for volume purchases, and multi-tier plans that provide higher co-payments from consumers for higher-priced brand-name drugs and lower co-payments from consumers for generic and other low-income substitutes. Also, the conversion of brand-name drugs from prescription to over-the-counter status has exerted some limited pressure to lower prices for consumers (Smith 2004, pp. 163–164). In the next section we explore these and other influences on drug pricing in more depth.

Confluence of Makers, Institutions, and Government on Drug Prices

There are many contenders for at least a share, if not the major share, of influence on drug distribution, access, and prices. This is evident in the current environment of institutions, markets, and government policies. We will resist the temptation to digress into a broad philosophical discourse on institutionalists, free market advocates, and those who espouse the use of government and its purse. Clearly, these philosophical differences have provided the "birthing rooms" for political and legislative deeds. Definitions of private goods, public goods, and quasi-public goods, as well as issues of efficiency, equity, and efficacy, were discussed in Chapter 2. These definitions and issues delineate the many parts of the *confluence* of forces affecting drug prices. In this section we will identify and explain how government policies can and do affect pharmaceutical pricing.

As identified earlier, government policies can distort some of the efficiency gains of markets. A free market exchange between a buyer and a seller results in either one or the other being better off and the other no worse off than before the exchange took place. Government policy can cause the price paid by the buyer or the price charged by the seller to change, which might eliminate or reduce the benefits of the free exchange. In pharmaceutical pricing, there is the clear and present change of the government reducing the price charged by the manufacturer or wholesaler to a level below the provider's return expected for innovation, risk, or high fixed costs. In turn, this could cause fewer new drugs and choices for consumers. Examples of those effects follow. In general, government policies, including taxation, could result in an excess burden of taxation. That is, the government would take more in taxes than society receives in benefits. Government policies could cause major redistributive effects on income. Those who contribute more in productive efforts would lose income to those who produce less.

The government may wish to reduce the number of senior citizens who are unable or unwilling to buy drugs at market prices. One method would be direct or indirect *price controls* as used in most other major nations. Recent research suggests that price controls, including reference pricing within categories of patent drugs, on "innovative drugs would have negative effects on industry structure and innovation" (Pammolli and Riccaboni 2004, p. 50). John E. Calfee outlines some of the problems inherent in price controls, including the "disincentives for research and development . . . and the inability of any controls system to handle the complex market activities that are essential to progress in the modern pharmaceutical research enterprise" (Calfee 2000, p. 45). Government policies on exports, imports, and reimportation of drugs can have major effects on pricing of drugs. A 2005 study in *Health Economics* predicted that reimportation could significantly reduce innovation and research in the pharmaceutical industry (Vernon 2005, pp. 1–16).

Buoyed by major international price differentials, consumers and state governments in the United States were attracted to drugs from Canada. Wholesalers and retailers were taking orders from suppliers in Europe, who gained profits from the "reimportation" of pharmaceutical products to the United States. These "imports" had the potential effect of transferring price controls to the United States. However, any legislative successes could be short-lived. Even though these efforts are rational, we should be aware of the "devastation price controls have brought to Europe's drug industry[;] . . . the American market now accounts for 62% of the global profit pool in the pharmaceutical business" ("Drug Wars" 2004, p. A14). As a result of price controls, European pharmaceutical companies have left Europe and have *not* grown. Some U.S. companies have made more generous foreign price policies as the prerequisite for a continuation of their supply of drugs to Europe. "Novartis itself has moved the center of its research operations to the United States from Europe . . ." ("Drug Wars" 2004, p. A14). The less expensive drugs imported from Canada and Europe into the United States could induce shortages of drugs in exporting countries. In December 2003, the Canadian International Pharmacy Association announced that its members will not provide drugs for proposed U.S. state and municipal employee and retiree programs because supplying such large-scale prescription purchasing plans would likely create drug shortages in Canada (Carlisle 2003, on-line pages). Pfizer, GlaxoSmithKline PLC, and Eli Lilly & Co. all have limited their sales of patent drugs to Canada. These actions are based on "concerns that the drugs are being re-exported to the U.S." (Carlisle 2003, on-line pages).

U.S. officials in the Department of Health and Human Services have reported that they will not offer guarantees that foreign source pharmaceuticals are safe since the drugs may not meet U.S. standards. Others are concerned about the counterfeiting of drugs. The Federal Drug Administration is attempting to devise methods to reduce drug costs for states as alternatives to the reexportation from Canada. These options would include "substitution of generics or comparable medicines, as well as group-purchase plans" (Mathews 2003, p. B6). Yet the temptation must be great: An October 27, 2003, report from the Illinois Department of Central Management reports potential savings of over $20 billion in co-payments and over $34 million in payments for prescription drug coverage for state employees if their health benefit program contracted purchases from Canadian pharmacies. Further, the report finds that there are similar methods in both the United States and Canada for regulating safety, ensuring efficacy, and preventing counterfeiting drugs ("Report on Feasibility" 2003, on-line pages).

In addition to the drug reexportation schemes with Canada, some states are using market mechanisms to reduce drug coverage premiums for state employees. In particular, the use of pharmacy benefit managers (PBMs) to negotiate discounts or rebates from pharmaceutical companies is a technique used by private industry. Some states have added their own savvy to alter the private industry arrangements with PBMs. West Virginia formed an alliance with six states. West Virginia also hired a pharmacy benefit manager that agreed to take an administrative fee rather than a profit. PBMs use a number of methods to reduce drug costs, including the classification of the prescribed drug within a group of similar lower-cost drugs (Waldholz 2002, on-line pages). Michigan uses a "preferred drug list" for its Medicaid program. Those pharmaceutical companies that reduce their prices stay on the list; those companies that will not reduce prices are removed from the list. Removal from the list usually results in loss of market share. These state programs are excellent examples of the combined use of market forces and a government willing to act as a catalyst for price and cost reductions (Waldholz 2002, on-line pages). Even though the examples cited are often those of states for their employees, the ability to use market mechanisms to become more efficient has an enabling function similar to the private sector. It is that same type of "muscle power" used by Wal-Mart to extract major cost savings from its suppliers. Wal-Mart's success has helped create and reflects the lower prices and competitiveness of the American economy. This function is central for policy decisions, particularly for pharmaceutical prices. If we think about the government as an agent of provision and the market as the principal producer of drugs, it becomes incumbent for government to seek the lowest possible prices for consumers while *not* unduly lowering the incentives for producers to assume risks, including high fixed costs. At this juncture of markets and government, it may be instructive to look at the fundamentals of the behavior of profit-maximizing pharmaceutical firms. We will counterface this behavior with some facts about the consumers.

Pharmaceutical firms are fairly competitive when considered in the aggregate. In 1992, "583 firms exist in the U.S. pharmaceutical industry. The largest four firms account for 25 percent of industry output, and the largest eight are responsible for 42 percent. The Herfindahl-Hirschman index of market concentration is very low at 341" (Santerre and Neun 2000, p. 509). However, if we examine separate therapeutic markets, for example, cardiovasculars, antibiotics, diabetic therapy, psychostimulants, and so forth, we find that these markets exhibit higher levels of concentration. Taking the largest four firms in each of these separate therapeutic markets, with their percentage of market sales, we find concentration ratios of 46 to 86 percent (Santerre and Neun 2000, p. 5). A more careful examination of those firms indicates that firms make most of their profits from a few "blockbuster" and perennial favorite drugs.

Much of what goes on in pharmaceutical markets is rational. Pharmaceutical firms have very high fixed costs: on average, from $600 to

$800 million to develop a drug on its path from discovery to market. Given these costs and relatively low variable costs, pharmaceutical firms practice what is known as "price discrimination." Price discrimination is the practice of charging different customers different prices for the same product. Once a firm receives a patent, it acts like a monopolist that continues to sell additional drugs as long as price is greater than marginal cost. This becomes the avenue for price discrimination. If the firm can separate its customers into different groups or markets, it will likely charge the highest possible price for each group. The challenge is to discover the price sensitivity or price elasticity of demand for each group. The price discrimination will be as successful as long as the following conditions or criteria are sustainable (these are not always mutually exclusive criteria):

1. There are differing price elasticities* of demand among the different buyers or groups of buyers for the same product. Thus, the firm may not be able or willing to charge senior citizens the same prices as for citizens under age sixty-five. The drug firms know that they can offer discount cards (now part of Medicare) to seniors and low-income people because of their greater sensitivity to prices. As long as the firms are able to generate higher revenue with relatively high prices for most sales (inelastic price elasticity) in the United States while increasing the volume of sales to compensate for lower prices for low-income, elderly, and people living in the nations with price controls (relatively elastic), total revenue will increase. In other words, if a pharmaceutical company can charge prices greater than marginal costs for most American customers and thus increases revenue and profits, the firm can afford to offer lower prices to Canadians and others as long as the prices cover variable costs.

*Price elasticity of demand is defined as

$$\frac{percent\ change\ in\ quantity\ (Q)\ demanded}{percent\ change\ in\ price\ (P)}$$

For an elastic demand response, there would be more than a proportional change of quantity demanded to the change in price, resulting in the value of the ratio > 1. For inelastic response, the value of the ratio would be < 1.

2. The sellers must be able to sell in separate markets. This follows the previous criterion and is essential to price discrimination. Do not ask your friend, relative, or neighbor what he or she is paying for pharmaceutical products if you are paying a standard price. These separate drug markets are at the very center of the current pricing controversy. As described in the first condition for price discrimination, these separate markets allow price discrimination. If Canada, Europe, and the United States are separate markets, higher prices in one market with high volume and relatively inelastic demand (U.S.) creates the bulk of profits and revenue. The lower prices in Europe and Canada for American-produced drugs simply *add* to the profits generated in the United States if the prices cover variable costs. These costs are a small proportion of total costs compared to the very high fixed costs.

3. Buyers in one market *cannot* sell their purchases in a different market. This is what is at stake in the debate over reimportation or reexportation of drugs produced in the United States and sold in foreign nations for significantly lower prices. As we have explored earlier, these actions will impede price discrimination. Eventually, prices would be reduced in the United States as a result of foreign nations reexporting our drugs. Remember our earlier discussion of the inherent danger of these reexports on the innovation and research incentives for new drugs.

As much as price discrimination offends seniors and others facing large drug expenditures, they do support price discrimination in their favor, as with special discounted prices for transportation, entertainment, and early-bird dinners.

Price discrimination is rampant in the drug market, with different prices for large group buyers, wholesalers, large retail pharmacies, and small retail pharmacies ("Drug Price Program Notes" 2000, p. A18). Those large employers and others who use pharmacy benefit managers are able to negotiate major discounts for their costs of covering employees. The confluence of industry, insurance, managed care, and government on drug prices is complicated by a number of changing and unique conditions in the pharmaceutical industry. We discussed the uniqueness of the health care industry in Chapter 1. One unique condition is the asymmetry of information between providers of care and buyers. This condition often leads to the physician acting as the surrogate for the patient; that is, the physician makes decisions for the patient. This condition is compounded by the continuing and vast number of new chemical drugs and the relatively new explosion of biotechnology and bioinformatics. The latter is specially designed just to gather and analyze information about gene variations and computer-assisted design programs used in biotechnology. Many major pharmaceutical firms have created "alliances with many of these firms, and they will share the profit from any resulting drugs" (Bogner 1999, p. A14).

Profits and research funding take on new meaning in the twenty-first century. The recent struggle to create new blockbuster drugs is based on diminishing returns in the form of recent profit trends. In order to provide continuing research with streams of funding, the drug companies need new blockbuster drugs (Bogner 1999, p. A14). This need has been compromised by expiring patents. Merck announced in late 2003 that it would not meet 2003 earnings expectations as a result of depressed sales of some of its major drugs. The third-quarter reports for 2003 reflected problems in the form of expiring patents, few new blockbuster drugs, competition from generics, and new over-the-counter forms of brand-name drugs. Even though a one-quarter report is not indicative of past earnings and earnings potential, it does show that profits can rise and fall. More significantly for an analysis of the drug industry, the report demonstrates the relationship of brand-name drugs to the roles of competition, patents, and generics.

We have already discussed the role of international competition in drug prices, especially with respect to the reexportation of drugs. We are now experiencing a new form of foreign competition from India's pharmaceutical companies. These companies have emerged as important research units and have combined "their skill sets, which include excellent chemistry" with the result of "emerging as a credible force in the global pharmaceutical industry" (Slater 2003). Also, we now have university laboratories as well as entrepreneurial researchers who obtain patents and wait for the possibility of being a link to a new blockbuster drug and its profits (Landers 2004, pp. 1 and 11).

All of this has heightened the desire of drug firms to preserve patent extensions. Generic drug producers and consumers would be beneficiaries of restricting patents so that generics could be more competitive. Some governors of states have joined forces with businesses and labor unions to block patent extensions and to overhaul the 1984 Waxman-Hatch Act, which helped create the generics industry but also gave brand-name drugs some protection against generic competition (Adams and Harris 2002, p. A24). The need to allow greater competition, pressures on high prices, and the desire for greater access to drugs led to the Waxman-Hatch Act. The act extended the effective patent protection of 9 years (17 years in the law minus an average 8 years of clinic testing) by 5 years if the post-patent approval time is not more than 14 years. Under the act, generic competition was increased by allowing a generic drug to be approved with the proof that the "active ingredient is chemically identical to an approved drug and the blood levels in humans . . . are within statistical bounds (plus-or-minus 20 percent) imposed for the original drug. A torrent of generic drug approvals followed" (Scherer 1993, p. 100). By 2001, the "generics manufacturers' share of drugs sold, by volume, had risen to 49% from 19% for 1984" (Adams and Harris 2002, p. A24). Brand-name drug manufacturers have employed a number of tactics to delay the introduction of new generic drugs.

However, there does not appear to be a major effect of the increased shares of generics sold on the prices of brand-name drugs. F.M. Scherer attributes this outcome to two institutional factors. One is the tendency of physicians "to be risk-adverse, insensitive to cost, and creatures of habit, prescribing drugs by brand name even when much less expensive generic substitutes exist" (Scherer 1993, p. 101). Hospitals and managed care organizations have offset this tendency somewhat by the use of formularies (lists of generics and other low-cost drugs required for physician prescriptions). Managed care organizations, hospitals, other providers, and state-run health care organizations use the formularies for cost containment. With the end of anti-substitution laws in 1984, pharmacists can now substitute generic drugs even on prescriptions calling for brand-name drugs. Physicians and consumers do have the right to reject the generic or low-cost substitutes. However, most consumers and physicians, by omission or commission, leave the decision to substitute to the pharmacist. The pharmacist *may* decide based on his or her profit margins (Santerre and Neun 2000, p. 515). Thus, we might witness some increased effect of generic substitutes on the prices of brand-name drugs in the future. The other institutional factor identified by Scherer is that of consumer ignorance of the risks and inability or unwillingness to compare the relative effectiveness of generic drugs as compared to brand-name drugs (Scherer 1993, p. 101).

There have been some unsavory attempts on behalf of pharmaceutical companies to check the surge of generics into open competition with brand-name drugs. Some use court actions to forestall the generic entry into the market. Some brand-name drug companies have generated their own generic entry into competition with other generic manufacturers. In 1998, Zenith found a court challenge when it wanted to market its generic substitute for Abbott's Hytrik, which is used treat high blood pressure and prostate enlargement. An out-of-court deal was made on March 31, 1998, for Abbott to pay Zenith up to $2 million a month *not* to market its generic rival. Abbott also made a deal with Geneva Pharmaceuticals that it would be paid as much as $101 million *not* to produce a rival generic drug. With an ironic and further anti-competitive twist, Geneva and Abbott ended their agreement under pressure of an impending anti-trust action. This was just in time for Abbott to welcome terazozin as a generic substitute for its brand-name Hytrin (Stolberg and Gerth 2000b, on-line pages).

As the old song goes, "Nice work if you can get it, and you can get it if you try." As this new effort by major pharmaceutical companies to limit the competitive effects of generic drugs takes effect, we can expect price discrimination by firms. This might consist of a higher and more stable price for brand-name drugs and a lower and decreasing price for generic substitutes. Much depends on the information asymmetry between providers and users. The government could provide more information on chemical equivalence of brand-name and generic drugs as a public good. Also, to the extent that formularies and reference lists of drugs are used and required, this information will have powerful competitive and price reduction effects.

Some studies "suggest that both pre-patent and post-patent price competition often exists in pharmaceutical markets. The prices of both brand-name and generic products are found to be lower when a greater number of substitute products are available" (Santerre and Neun 2000, p. 528). Some perceive the mismeasurement of drug price indices as a critical factor in analyzing price increases. When generic drugs are included in the market basket of drug indices, they are entered as "new products in their own right, not as a lower-price substitution to some existing product. Thus *no* reduction in the index value accompanies their inclusion. . . . [T]his set of conventions implies an upward bias of about 1.2 percent per year in the measured Producer Price Index trend for drugs" (Scherer 1993, p. 102). Another bias is in the relative treatment of older branded drugs and the newer drugs. The older drugs tend to have higher prices, ceteris paribus, than the new products. However, the new products do not appear in the market basket of drugs until well after their initial market entry since the market basket changes infrequently. Thus, the index is biased upward, which results in a higher official rate of price increases than the rate shown by the records of the companies.

We have already discussed the need for profit in the pharmaceutical industry, and most studies verify a higher rate of profits than for other manufacturing firms. In 1997, the drug firms realized an after-tax return on equity of 23.2 percent compared to the 16.6 percent rate of all manufacturing firms in the same year; the after-tax return on assets was 9.5 percent for drug firms and 6.6 percent for all manufacturers (Santerre and Neun 2000, p. 545). However, many scholars caution us that these numbers belie the heavy innovation and research costs required. We remain convinced that this rate of return has made the United States the leader in pharmaceutical research and new products.

Other influences on drug prices include the role of insurance, which we will discuss more specifically in Chapters 5 and 7, on the uninsured and Medicare reform. Suffice it to say here that "insurance does more than just pay bills; it changes the amount and composition of bills . . . people generally use more, and more costly, medical goods and services when insurance covers their cost than when it does not" (Pauly 2004, p. 113). One additional influence of the government on pharmaceutical product availability and research is the Orphan Drug Act (1983). This act sought to increase incentives to produce drugs that would treat diseases that affected fewer than 200,000 people per year. Given the high cost of testing and the relatively few people over whom the fixed costs could be spread, Congress granted an exclusive right to market such a drug for seven years to the first firm to win approval. Over sixty orphan drugs were developed in the first nine years of the implementation of the law (Scherer 1993, p. 99).

Conclusion and Policy Implications

In order to provide an appropriate diagnosis of pharmaceutical pricing, we have identified the many separate forces that do affect decisions made by producers, wholesalers, retailers, government, insurers, and consumers. These separate forces include the market and its mechanisms, the government and its statues, industry and its institutional characteristics, and insurance and its effects on producers and consumers. It is important to note that none of these forces is independent or mutually exclusive of the others. It is the *confluence* of these forces that reveals how the market, government, and institutions vie with each other for dominance in issues of pricing, access, distribution, efficiency, and equity. In all of this, we observe that the market does have an important role to play in economizing on scarce resources, placing pressures on high prices, and finding the optimal or efficient outcomes. What is the combination of acceptable prices and availability of drugs for consumers that will also provide incentives for drug companies to continue research and innovation efforts? In all of the clamor about high prices for drugs, we need to identify and separate the effects of market mechanisms. If we do not allow market forces to operate, we may never know if we could have reduced prices of drugs and increased their availability. For example, the Medicare reform of 2003 provides for private insurance companies to compete with each other in both the issuance of drug discount cards (2004) and the pharmaceutical drug coverage (2006). Without this provision, we either would not know about any savings from competitive markets or we would have to use price controls, formularies, and limited access to drugs as policy devices. Would we be better off with price controls and less access to drugs? However, market mechanisms need some control, especially with relatively high rates of return on equity and with the need to assure access to drugs for people with low incomes. How about some combination of markets and government? For example, we might consider the government issue of vouchers or credits for low-income people. Beginning in June 2004, the U.S. federal government issued $600 credits toward drug discount cards for low-income seniors. All of these policy directions must consider the special and unique characteristics of the pharmaceutical industry. In the United States, there is a bold experiment under way. It is an attempt unlike in any other nation to envelope markets, government, and institutions in a cooperative venture.

4

Managed Care

Revolution, Evolution, or Devolution?

The Setting

Spending in the United States on hospital care alone reached $451.2 billion in 2001. The total expenditure for hospital care in 1965 was $13.8 billion. The total health care expenditures were $1,424.5 billion in 2001 compared with $188.7 billion (in 2001 dollars) in 1965 (U.S. House, Ways and Means 2003, Table C-2, p. C4). When managed care became dominant in the 1990s, inflation in health care grew at a much lower rate than previously. Prior to managed care the government (both federal and state) used a variety of cost control and, later, prospective payment schemes to contain health care inflation. Managed care proved its effectiveness largely through market forces. These negotiated markets allowed some give-and-take to find prices or reimbursement rates that satisfied both providers and the firms that carried most of the burden for their employees' health insurance premiums. This was clearly a triumph for the role of private insurance and prices set in the market as opposed to being administered by governments. There are criticisms of the managed care organizations, but few could doubt its successes with discounting providers' prices. This chapter traces the origins of managed care and sets forth its various forms. Report cards are then issued on the effectiveness of managed care with respect to price inflation, utilization, physician incomes, and medical technology and its costs.

Managed Care Organizations: The Who and What

Managed care organizations (MCOs) usually consist of two types of organizations and a hybrid. These are really insurance and reimbursement plans. Two types are health maintenance organizations (HMOs) and preferred provider organizations (PPOs). Point-of-service (POS) differs only mechanically from PPOs and HMOs.

In HMOs, enrollees (members) subscribe to a plan that not only insures them for any health care services covered by the plan but also guarantees them health care twenty-fou: hours a day, seven days a week. This guarantee reverses the economics of health care in that it places some financial accountability on hospitals and physicians. Since the fees from subscribers comprise the largest source of income for HMOs, it became prudent for the physicians and hospitals to reduce costs. Hospitals are the most extensive users of relatively scarce health care resources, including registered nurses, physicians (on staff, including hospital employed pathologists, etc.), buildings, other facilities, diagnostic and radiological equipment, and emergency rooms. Some of these scarce resources must be used inefficiently, as in the example of emergency rooms, which are often underutilized. They need to be available in the event of situations that require enough space for a mini-disaster and qualified professional medical personnel. The space and equipment must be adequate even if they are underutilized under normal conditions. HMOs cut costs by providing alternatives to hospitalization, reducing length of stay for patients, using same-day surgeries, testing *before* patients arrive for health care, and using less invasive surgical techniques.

The incentive for all of these lower-cost programs is the desire to produce profits or, for not-for-profit hospitals, to generate surpluses. These reductions in the use of relatively scarce resources that carry high price tags are highly desirable from an economic viewpoint. Microeconomic efficiency includes the allocation of scarce resources to their most productive (efficient) and desired uses given the constraints of income and prices. Thus, there is an efficiency gain when we can produce a given amount of medical services with a revenue or income cap at lower costs. However, since consumers are not sovereign in terms of the quantity of care and the types and extensions of care, less than the full flexibility is expected in freely functioning markets. Indeed, since HMOs are the least flexible plans in managed care, they have become less popular than the more flexible PPOs and POS programs. In a survey conducted by the SMG Marketing Group and the Kaiser Family Foundation, patients found HMOs less flexible than PPOs or POS plans. Sixty-one percent of the survey respondents reported that HMO physicians have decreased the amount of time for a patient visit. Sixty-three percent reported that HMOs made referrals to specialists more difficult, and 50 percent felt that HMOs actually decrease the quality of care for ill patients. Over 30 percent of these survey respondents reported difficulties in receiving sufficient information from their health plans and in having the plan pay for emergency room service. Consequently, this inflexibility has resulted in a much slower increase in enrollment for HMOs than PPOs (Freudenheim 2000a, p. B4).

The PPOs are much more flexible than HMOs. The PPOs are much more closely related to and compatible with market mechanisms, particularly prices and quantities of market exchanges. However, we should not expect complete consumer sovereignty given the uniqueness of health care markets, incomplete and asymmetric information, and contracts that resemble collective bargaining agreements. PPOs are a major form of managed care. Major health plans negotiate discounted prices from physicians and hospitals. These prices become available to employers whose employees are required to enroll in these programs. These preferred physicians and hospitals expect that the large number of plan members will more than compensate for the reduced per-unit charge for services. This feature becomes operative in the market if there are competitors. Much of what is happening in health care reform is dependent on competition. If market type reforms are to be compatible with government initiatives, competition among insurers will test the ability of the private sector to be a viable partner (see Chapter 7, on Medicare reform). One distinguishing feature of PPOs is flexibility. Negotiated markets in which PPOs function allow buyers of medical services to bargain with sellers or providers for prices of services *to be delivered* in the near future. The ensuing contracts reflect the relative demand for these services and the relative supply *if* there are competing PPOs. The PPOs negotiate the price discounts based in part on the expected volume of patients. So, if the price paid to a physician is decreased by 5 percent but the volume of patients increases by 7 percent, the physician's total revenue increases at least in respect to the managed care patients.

The PPOs arrange the prices and types of services prospectively but pay after the services are rendered. This usually requires the submitting of forms by the employee or member of the plan. The employee of the human resources department must match the claim with the response of the insurance company (MCO) and pay or settle any differences. Bureaucracy and paperwork are often major sources of disaffection for the plans. The point-of-service plan is a hybrid of a PPO and an HMO. It more closely resembles and usually functions in the same manner as a PPO. Employers contract with a major health plan (MCO) to provide health care coverage for their employees at discounted prices from a designated network of hospitals and physicians. The distinguishing difference between a PPO and a POS plan is that any paperwork and co-payment is completed at the time of the service to the patient. Typically, the patient makes any co-payment to the physician office at the time of the visit. The patient does *not* have to complete any claim form for the MCO plan or human resource department. For hospital and out-patient services, the PPO has already negotiated a contract with the hospital to provide services at a discount. For example, if a hospital bills its services as $3,000 and the PPO has negotiated a 10 percent discount, the patient will receive a bill for $300 from the hospital. There are no claim forms to complete; there is only a $300 check to send to the hospital. Most patients are pleased with this arrangement.

Some employers offer a choice to their employees. In addition to a PPO, HMO, or POS plan, the employer may offer the employee a free choice of providers, albeit at a high employee contribution to the total benefit package. There are a number of issues related to choice, which is dependent on the ability of competing forms of health care delivery. In all of the forms of managed care, there is a limited network of providers. With HMOs, there is a closed panel of physicians available to consumers. This limited choice of physicians is much more restricted in highly structured HMOs, in which the physicians form a group. This group has a separate accounting and legal identity from that of the HMO plan. The physicians are salaried and can share profits of the overall plan or incur some of the losses. The prototype of this kind of highly structured plan is the Kaiser-Permanente HMO, which originated as a program for employees of the Kaiser Industries in the 1940s. The physicians' group was known as Permanente. As other HMOs adopted this design, it became known as the staff plan. A less structured form is known as the independent or individual practice association (IPA). This plan allows physicians to treat patients on a fee-for-service basis. Sometimes, the IPA form allows the physician to continue to treat patients who are *not* subscribers to the HMO. Other HMOs have contractual arrangements to pay physicians on a capitation basis, that is, a fixed amount for each subscriber who receives treatment.

Health maintenance organizations and other forms of preferred provider organizations have been used as cost-cutting competitive devices by governments, including the federal government's Medicare choice programs. The first phase of the Choice Program was authorized by the Congress in 1982. Medicare beneficiaries could choose to enroll in managed care organizations that accept risk contracts. The MCOs that take part in this arrangement agree to accept a per subscriber payment or capitation, provided that the MCOs provide the same coverage of health care services as in the regular Medicare program. However, the attraction for Medicare enrollees was that many of those contracts provide extra services including routine physical examinations (97 percent of the plans), eye examinations (92 percent), ear examinations (78 percent), out-patient drugs (68 percent), and immunizations (89 percent). These figures were for 1997. The risk contracts gave the providers an opportunity to maximize profits by careful avoidance or limitation of adverse risk and by acceptance of low-risk enrollees (Aaron 1999, pp. 40–41). The Balanced Budget Act of 1997 increased the number of alternatives for Medicare beneficiaries, including medical savings accounts (MSAs) and provider-sponsored organizations (PSOs). These alternatives are now packaged as the Medicare + Choice program (Aaron 1999, p. 43). Additional programs and choices, including prescription drug coverage, became available with major Medicare reform in late 2003. These and other features are discussed in Chapter 7, on Medicare.

Another example of how managed care can produce significant savings in costs and allow more choice for participants is the successful efforts by the City of Milwaukee. Here is a situation in which a government can function to provide health insurance coverage for its employees that utilizes market forces. The connection between choice, market forces, competition, and reduced costs is considerable. If, at the same time, consumer welfare is improved (gains to consumers are greater than costs), economists would generally pronounce that the outcome is positive. The Milwaukee plan is named the Employee Health Plan; the idea for the plan came from the mayor of the city, John O. Norquist (Riemer 1990, pp. 15–16). The plan offers employees of the city a variety of HMO plans and its own standard indemnity plan. The city plan gives its employees a free choice of providers, physicians, and hospitals. This plan has a deductible and a limited coverage of health care services. The competing HMOs submit bids that meet the standards of the city for benefit coverage and for financial stability. The employees can choose among any HMO that meets the city's standards or the standard city indemnity plan. The city will pay the entire cost of the lowest-bidding HMO plan. If an employee selects any other HMO plan or the city plan that exceeds 105 percent of the lowest-bidding HMO plan, the employee will pay part or all of the extra cost. The system has worked since it encourages competing HMO plans to reduce premiums and it encourages employees to be cost conscious and partial risk bearers.

The theme that emerges from many, if not all, of the issues explored in this book is that competition and market forces can be unleashed to promote the general welfare if they are properly and intelligently guided by government. One of the reasons that managed care became viable in the health care industry is that it was the conduit for the market mechanism to express its demand for and supply of health care. MCOs could and did negotiate a price for health care services between providers and large-volume buyers. At the same time, MCOs could determine the value at the margin of additional services by setting a cap on the number of days of care and influencing decisions for same-day surgeries. MCOs effectively manipulated the market in their self-interest of profits. But in so doing, they were largely responsible for lower inflation for health care services in the mid-1990s.

The Evolution of Managed Care: The Humble Beginnings

One can think of how consumers (they used to be called "patients") enter the health care system. Given the unique features of the system (see Chapter 1), the consumer depends upon the physician for information such as health condition diagnosis, prognosis, and prescription. This description fits the pre–managed care days but also continues to serve as the major entry point for health care services. Before we explore the constraints on and modifications of this system, we might dwell on its professional and consumer charter. If guided by the Hippocratic oath, the physician would render the best possible advice and care to the patient. Before the 1950s, there was little insurance or other external financing available for the care given by physicians. So it was a two-party deal for the most part. Access to physician care was constrained by its cost and the incomes of consumers. One had to be willing and able to pay the price for care. Private health care was a private good with the exclusion principle working in almost full form: Those who were unwilling or unable to pay the price for physician care were excluded from its benefits.

Before we judge this system as totally insensitive to the poor and catastrophically ill, note that there were a number of charity and clinical services available in public and urban settings. Some physicians would have a sliding scale schedule of fees that were inversely rated to high-income patients. That is, those patients with low incomes would pay less than those with higher incomes; sometimes, physicians would not bill the very poor. But the physician's "black bag" had a much lower cost attached for the doctor. The general practitioner (GP) had few diagnostic tools or machines, relatively simple paperwork, and other than a registered nurse and perhaps a receptionist, was not assisted by a plethora of paraprofessionals, technicians, and billing personnel. The medical doctor did not have to wait until payment came from a third party such as an insurance company or government agency. General practitioners usually worked in solo practice. Specialists were rarely available or consulted. Obviously, cases calling for surgery or involving serious traumas or certain illnesses would be referred to others. Second opinions from other doctors were rarely sought. Under these circumstances, entry to medical care either from a medical doctor or a hospital was constrained by the price tags of the services. Price became the "regulator" for the flow of patients to the physician or hospital. Health care was rationed on the bases of prices and incomes. Health insurance was rare until the 1950s and existed mostly in the form of indemnity payments for hospital care. Medicare and Medicaid did not arrive until the mid-1960s. Moreover, insurance played the primary role of helping finance health care. Most hospital care was in the form of community not-for-profit hospitals. Physicians and clinics were identified as givers of primary care. Hospitals were at the secondary level, and medical centers were at the tertiary level of care. Although physicians enjoyed staff privileges at hospitals that sent special case patients to medical centers, there was little, if any, vertical integration of the three levels of care. Hospitals were essentially autonomous institutions of care and had little concern for horizontal integration. While these organizational structures may have lacked economies of scale efficiencies, they were not extracting rents or excessive surpluses sometimes associated with current consolidations of hospitals.

At this stage in the development of managed care, insurance was still a financier rather than an allocator of health care resources or a major determinant of decisions on the what, how, how much, when, and for whom to produce health care questions. Before the 1950s, private health insurance paid for only about 10 percent of all medical costs (Dranove

2002, p. 48). In the 1950s, hospital insurance began to emerge as a major source of indemnifying losses associated with hospital care. Group plans were developed primarily as an employee benefit due to the economies of volume purchases and the law of large numbers; the latter would allow actuaries to develop plans that would spread the effects of adverse risk selection (the buying of insurance by those with the high-risk profiles) among a large group of insured. Hospital administrators formed the Blue Cross insurance system as a means to finance increasingly costly hospital stays. Little attention, if any, was given to out-patient, clinic, or ambulatory care since these forms of care were not in high demand and since the major costs of health care were to be found in hospitals. Later, Blue Shield organizations were developed by physicians to provide financing for patients using physician services. These early Blues were formed in state and regional organizations. Their reimbursements were paid retrospectively, that is, after the service was rendered. Many physician members of Blue Shield would accept, as full payment for their services, the rate determined in advance by Blue Shield. Other physicians would ask for additional payments from the patients. Both Blue Cross and Blue Shield were not-for-profit organizations. Only in recent years have some "Blues" converted to for-profit status. Again, the emphasis was indemnity payments without interference with the decisions of individual physicians and hospitals. In more recent years the Blue Cross and Blue Shield organizations have combined their boards under a common organizational structure. The Blues now provide health insurance for 33 percent of Americans (Fuhrmans 2004b, on-line pages).

Most of the hospital structure of autonomous physicians and not-for-profit community hospitals lasted through the 1960s. An important change in the reimbursement occurred in 1965 with the introduction by the Congress of Medicare, a federally financed program of medical insurance for those over the age of sixty-five with some exceptions for others; for example, Medicare eventually covered kidney dialysis for people over sixty-five *and* under sixty-five. Also in 1965, Medicaid was passed into law. Financed jointly by the federal, state, and local governments, Medicaid was introduced into law to cover the indigent population for health care. Both of these programs increased the demand for health care, with the consequent increase in health care costs and exacerbated supply shortages. These new forms of insurance coverages were still based primarily on inpatient hospital stays.

Hospitals use the most expensive health care resources including highly skilled physicians and nurses, in addition to advanced medical technology. As this evolution to managed care unfolds, we begin to see how emerging market forces take on these expensive users of resources. So, the old structures created high costs to engender various attempts at restraining those costs. The attempts to economize caused changes in the structure, conduct, and performance of the health care industry. In the 1960s, retrospective reimbursement systems based on indemnity payments were still dominant.

The retrospective payment (after the illness or accident costs were determined by the hospital) appeared to be having an effect of increasing the premiums for health care insurance, almost as if the insurance carriers were giving blank checks to the hospitals for the covered services. Then the notion of prospective reimbursement arrived. New York became the first state (1970) to have an "all-payer, prospective payment, rate-setting system" (Dranove 2002, p. 49). All of those adjectives are important. Being an all-payer plan meant the end to cost shifting. Before the change to a new system, hospitals would often shift costs from lower-paying insurers such as Blue Cross or Medicaid to higher-paying insurers such as commercial insurance companies. Of course, the all-payer system would later break down under the pressure of managed care. The prospective part of the scheme is the major change. This means that the payment for services is determined in advance of any incidence of illness or other basis for hospital care. The whole nature of insurance changes from indemnity for loss that is actuarially determined to a system that challenges the costs claimed by the patient or hospital. It strongly suggests that the hospital should and could control its costs if confronted by prospective payment schemes. The interesting part comes from the use of rate setting by the individual states. To an economist who had a front-row seat on the action as a member of a board of directors of an upstate New York hospital, the system appeared to provide disincentives for efficiency and rewards for the best game strategy. This cost-based system depended heavily on the ability and political will of state governments to establish reimbursement rates that reflected the values of services rendered.

That means that providers, hospitals, and physicians need to be paid their explicit or implicit costs or else their supply of services is reduced or moves elsewhere. Implicit costs include what could have been earned elsewhere, or the opportunity costs incurred by the supplier in forgoing other occupations or sources of revenue. The patient or consumer wants a price or reimbursement rate that is affordable and is commensurate with the benefits of the services, particularly at the margin of that next or last unit of the service. The next question is the major consideration: Can government establish those rates or prices better than some market or market-like mechanism? Part of the evolution to managed care witnessed a major role for government that was severely reduced in the 1980s when a number of market forces were introduced. Some strange things happened on the way to more market-led efficiencies. We discovered that the all-payer prospective reimbursement scheme had inadvertently led to higher costs of health care. The New York State prospective all-payer system (1970–85) was named the New York State Prospective Hospital Reimbursement Methodology (NYPHRM). This system, like many other state systems, was based on costs that were passed through from the provider to the consumers and insurance companies via reimbursement rates. The basic formula for the New York State system was as follows for each hospital:

$$\frac{allowable\ costs}{patients\ days} = per\ diem\ reimbursement\ rate$$

The game behind this scheme was played by hospitals wanting to have the highest possible budget or allowable costs and the lowest possible number of patient-days (the number of patients times the average length of stay, or ALOS). In other words, the CEO or CFO of the hospital wanted the highest possible value of the ratio. The higher the value of the ratio, the higher would be the per diem reimbursement rate. The state agency would exert downward pressures on the size of the budget. It would want to have the number of patient days that actually developed and *not* a number that allowed hospitals a higher-than-justified reimbursement rate. The allowable costs were based on the norm for a group of hospitals in a region with similar characteristics such as number of beds and mix of services. A "normal" competitive cost per day for the region was determined as the basis for the allowable budget of a particular hospital. When this system began, our hospital in Ithaca, New York, was a county hospital whose employees were part of the New York State pension program. The program had relatively high contributions required of its public hospitals. It was a benefits-determined plan rather than a contributions-determined plan. This arrangement was complicated by the fact that many of the employees of the hospital would leave the system prior to being fully vested or eligible to receive pension funds upon retirement. These "leavers" were not able to transfer the funds to any employment outside the state. In effect, this benefit-determined plan meant that the Ithaca hospital was subsidizing the pension funds of public employees elsewhere in the state. This in turn meant that the Ithaca hospital had higher than normal pension costs. Consequently, the hospital received less in its allowable budget than its costs. Appeals to the state agency for special consideration were denied. It is not in the scope of this book to provide the details of other adjustments made to the operating budget. Score a victory for the state if one is keeping score! On the denominator of the ratio, patient-days, there was room for game playing. Hospitals might deliberately report lower patient-days than those actually recorded. All other factors being constant, this action would cause the hospital to receive a higher per diem reimbursement. This additional revenue could be banked in the short-term market for an interest income gain. However, if the state auditor discovered this underreporting, it would assess an adjustment charge on the hospital. The adjustment charge would be based on the per diem reimbursement rate that would have resulted from the actual patient-day count. The hospital would often still come out ahead since the revenue from the short-term market usually exceeded the adjustment charge.

A more significant outcome of the NYPHRM system would happen if a more efficient hospital with a lower average length of stay received a lower per diem rate than a hospital with a higher ALOS, especially given the nature of high fixed costs and a front-loading of costs (higher per day costs in the first few days of a hospital stay). Suppose the data in Table 4.1 exist for two different hospitals. Table 4.1 shows two fictional hospitals, "A" and "B," which are faced with the same per day costs and are allowed same per diem reimbursement. To simplify this hypothetical example, the patients in each hospital have identical profiles with the same diagnoses. Hospital A has the longer average length of stay, eight days, while Hospital B has a shorter average length of stay, five days. Hospital A may justify or rationalize its longer stays on the basis that longer stays produce more total revenue ($2,400 > $1,500) and more net revenue ($640 > $40). However, Hospital B is more efficient than Hospital A. That is, the cost of entire episode of illness for patients and other payers is $1,460 at Hospital B, which is $300 less than the $1,760 tab at Hospital A. Because of the biases in the medical care component

Table 4.1

Per Diem Reimbursement and Hospital Costs

Hospital A: 8-Day Stay*

Day #	1	2	3	4	5	6	7	8	Totals
Per diem reimbursement ($)**	300	300	300	300	300	300	300	300	$2,400
Costs per day ($)	400	330	300	250	180	100	100	100	$1,760
Net revenue ($)	−100	−30	0	50	120	200	200	200	$640

Hospital B: 5-Day Stay*

Day #	1	2	3	4	5	Totals
Per diem reimbursement ($)**	300	300	300	300	300	$1,500
Costs per day ($)	400	330	300	250	180	$1,460
Net revenue ($)	−100	−30	0	50	120	$40

*Same per day costs for both hospitals.
**All numbers are hypothetical.

of the consumer price index, Hospital B's average cost per day of $292 would represent a difference of over 32 percent in *per day* costs compared to the $220 cost per day of Hospital A. Hospital administrators would prefer the greater total revenue and lower per day average cost of Hospital A. However, if we look at the economic impact of Hospital A, we discover that its program increases the cost of care in terms of scarce resources used and in opportunity costs of production forgone.

This economic analysis discloses a key element in estimating total expenditures when government agency controls the per day rate of reimbursement (in effect, the price) and the hospital has some control over the quality. If price times quantity equals total expenditures, the hospital will attempt to manipulate quantity to its advantage, which may well be to the disadvantage of society. Both price and quantity supplied or demanded are significant elements in the economics of the firm. Theory would tell us that if the price of a particular hospital service increases, ceteris paribus, hospitals would be willing to supply more of the service. So, if the state agency increases the per day rate of reimbursement and decreases or does not sufficiently increase payments for out-patient services, we may expect that in-patient care will increase whenever it is a viable alternative to out-patient care. As more and more out-patient services are developed and are not covered completely by state formularies and insurance, hospitals increased the prices for those services.

This misallocation of resources triggered by the government obsession with costs appears in many government-run health systems. The resources (human capital and technology) flow to their payment sources. After decades of inefficiency and emigration of M.D.s and R.N.s from the National Health Service in the United Kingdom, the Tories experimented with funds given to physicians and hospitals. These internal market reforms allowed the health service providers to direct the resources to where the patients were going. This revolutionary idea merely replicates a free market in which the pounds sterling would follow the patients. At the risk of oversimplification and of ignoring unique institutional factors, this issue is at the base of the government and market dichotomy.

During this period (1970–mid-1980s), the state-run health care systems in the United States failed to control costs, particularly for the relatively high resource costs for hospitals. Indeed, the New York State–administered system allowed the two-year-old costs of hospitals to be trended forward with respect to hospital inflation. Those hospitals that failed to control these costs were *rewarded* with a higher per day reimbursement rate. Those hospitals that exercised some control in these costs were *penalized* with a lower rate of reimbursement. It became clear that the state control of the price (reimbursement rate) variable led hospitals to exploit the quantity (ALOS) variable. Even at that, the states followed with a variety of volume adjustments such as the example identified earlier. In turn, this was followed by manipulation of volume by some hospital executives. Anyone who is familiar with the command economy and state plans of the now defunct Soviet Union would understand the futility of these schemes.

New Directions: Diagnostic Related Groups

The next major change (mid-1980s–1996) in this evolution to managed care was the institution of diagnostic related groups (DRGs) for Medicare hospital stays and the similar case-mix payment systems of the states for other patients. This was to be a system that put caps on *revenue* rather than on costs. The logic was that if revenue was based on competitive costs of hospitals, then hospitals would now have some market variables for use in decision making. In competitive markets, firms are price takers. That is, the firm must charge the going price that is set in the market by all buyers and sellers of a similar product or service. This sets up the discipline of the market. Each firm has to determine how much of the product to produce and sell; it wants to maximize profits. Usually the firm will maximize profits at the optimal output at which marginal cost = marginal revenue. To do this, the firm has control of its costs at least to the level of competing firms. If the firm cannot sufficiently control its costs, it may leave the market, reduce its output, or enter a different market. This competitive model has much in common with DRGs. If we consider the DRG payments as the price for a particular disease category (over 400 diagnostic related groups), then a hospital has its payment (price) determined in advance of the incidence of illness or accident. The hospital is a "price taker." It must have its costs equal to or less than the DRG payment. If its costs exceed the DRG payment, the hospital would have to incur the difference as a loss. If the costs were lower than the payment, the hospital would realize a profit or a surplus (not-for-profit hospitals). Each disease category had a separate payment code. These DRG payments were based on costs for similar hospitals. The more a hospital reduced its costs or increased its efficiency, the more profitable it would become. This suggests that under competitive pressures, scarce resources in hospitals could be economized. This is exactly what the theory and practice have been in the market economies. So, the ratio of DRG payment to costs becomes the operative basis to release market forces.

When the system began, there was an allowance for hospital-specific costs for a portion of the DRG payment. This was done to allow hospitals time to adjust to the new system. Eventually, the DRG payment became the competitive norm. The notion was to allow adjustment but not to support bad cost habits just as tariffs might support high cost forms in international trade.

This DRG system as applied to the states was known by a variety of names. It was known in New York State as the Case Payment System (CPS), sometimes referred to as a case-mix scheme. As noted earlier, the CPS in New York State developed in the mid-1980s; 1996 was the last year for the NYPHRM all-payer system. It was replaced by the January 1, 1997, Health Care Reform Act (HCRA), which we will discuss later in this chapter. The CPS was based, as in the federal DRGs, on payments per diagnostic category. This state program determined payment for all payers except for Medicare (federal DRGs). However, the weights for the New York program differed from those of the federal system. The CPS payments per diagnostic category were based on service intensity weights (SIWs). The commissioner for New York State had the authority to determine the blend of the hospital-specific and group (norm) average for the payment rates. In 1988, 90 percent of the payment rate was for hospital-specific costs; in 1989 and 1990, the hospital-specific weights were 75 and 45 percent, respectively.

This fundamental change in the insurance reimbursement system to a genuine prospective payment system with payment caps had an impressive record of lowering costs and reallocating resources. For example, many hospitals looked at the most favorable DRG or case-mix categories and began to specialize in those areas of care. If eye surgery or cardiology care were profitable, hospitals began to specialize in those areas. Humana Hospital Lucerne in Orlando, Florida, is an example of a hospital that chose to specialize in bypass surgeries, angioplasties, and cardiac catherizations (Burda 1988, p. 30). This for-profit hospital increased its share of Medicare patients and "had a pretax profit of $9.4 million on revenues of $62 million" (Burda 1988, p. 30). As Medicare DRG payments were scheduled to decline, the hospital took advantage of rising OB/GYN payments with a new OB/GYN facility (Burda 1988, p. 30). However, some hospitals could not make the adjustments due to limited patient service areas, high union costs for labor, and limited capacity. Consequently, some hospitals reduced their staff and used other cost-cutting methods. Still others closed down or shared services with former competitors. New hospitals began to think in terms of fewer hospitals and smaller hospitals. Those hospitals that were relatively more efficient than others would often have lower average length of stay. These hospitals were favored in a DRG system that included a competitive ALOS in its formula. A 1996 report from the New York State Department of Health stated that "Tompkins County's per capita hospital costs are the lowest of any county in the entire state of New York" ("The New York Health Care Reform Act" 1997, pp. 4–5). Cayuga Medical Center is the only hospital in Tompkins County. The hospital had the lowest ALOS for many years. This ALOS worked to the disadvantage of the hospital during the old per-day reimbursement scheme even though it was representative of efficiency. The hospital now benefited from having lower costs than the norm under the Medicare and state DRG system.

The DRG, or prospective payment system, worked well to foster, if not force, hospitals to function more efficiently with a mix of government-set rates and a dosage of market forces. However, government-set rates simply did not adjust well to the changing dimensions of institutions, delivery systems, less invasive operations, new technology, and a new emphasis on out-patient care. The market was represented but not allowed to function to its potential. Much of what our nation experienced in health care price and cost regulation was focused on in-patient care. Even though capital costs were essentially "passed through" from the technology procedures to the insurance companies, there was no real attempt to assess the value of the diffusion of the technological advances on the costs and benefits of medical care. This would be left to managed care.

Under Medicare, physicians had been reimbursed under "the usual-customary-reasonable (UCR) or the customary-prevailing-and-reasonable (CPR) method" (Santerre and Neun 2000, p. 359). These methods were designed to prevent physicians from overcharging patients in order to take advantage of the government payment. However, many physicians simply inflated their fee schedule for all patients; therefore, they were still charging the customary and prevailing fee for Medicare patients. In 1992, as the result of the Omnibus Budget Reconciliation Act (OBRA) of 1989, a new Resource-based Relative Value Scale System (RBRVS) was instituted. This "system of fees considers the time and effort of physician resources, necessary to produce physician services" (Santerre and Neun 2000, p. 359). The new system rewarded time-consuming services such as primary care relative to surgical procedures. The underlying value scale provided about a half of the basis for Medicare payments, with the other half made up of expense-related payments. Some critics of the RBRVS system contend that there is insufficient inclusion of shifts in demand and supply for physicians and the consequent changes in input values (Santerre and Neun 2000, pp. 359–361). An ambiguous feature of the Medicare reimbursement program for physicians is that of the right of Medicare patients to enter into private contracts with physicians for services. Under Medicare, the government had attempted to restrict this right. In spite of the Clinton administration's attempts to retain the restrictions, the U.S. Court of Appeals for the District of Columbia ruled that there was no prohibition on private contracts. Physicians would be allowed to accept payments from patients for services considered "unreasonable" by the government. Also, private contracts would be allowed for services that were not reimbursed in Medicare; these would include cosmetic and experimental procedures ("A Victory for Private Medicine" 1999, p. A26). Apparently, there is a mind-set that suggests any more of a health care service for some means less for others. The counter to this thesis is that the extra private services represent *more* care for some without any diminution of services for others. This is another example of where the free market complements government services to allow people more choices than would be available under a government single-payer system.

Managed Care Takes on the Government: The Revolution

Managed care has its origins in many prepaid, company-sponsored programs for employees and public employees dating back to the early 1900s. However, the emergence of health maintenance organizations (HMOs) as contenders for a role in health care decisions began with Kaiser Industries and its Kaiser Foundation Health Plan at the end of World War II. This plan was not identified as an HMO until 1970, although Kaiser Industries had earlier built medical and hospital facilities for its employees in a prepaid group practice (Dranove 2002, pp. 38–39). The HMOs that were described earlier in this chapter grew slowly in the 1960s and 1970s. However, in the 1980s HMO enrollments increased by 23 million to reach 33 million enrollees by 1990. By 2000, there were over 60 million enrollees and over 500 HMOs. By the same year, 80 percent of American workers were in a managed care plan.

An important drama began as managed care developed lower rates of hospital reimbursement than did state governments under the prospective payment system (PPS) or its alternate names of DRGs and case-mix payment schemes. (The DRGs were really the province of the federal Medicare program.) The managed care system worked since both the price and quantity of health care to be delivered were negotiable. The market forces are much more operative under managed care. This is a *negotiated market* arrangement. Although it is not a free market, it does allow sellers (providers) to offer a price and quantity of services to buyers (mainly employers for employee health plan) through a managed care organization (HMO, PPO, or POS). The MCO arranges a discounted price with the providers so that business firms can offer these benefits to their employees. Managed care simply got our attention in the United States as a viable vehicle for the virtues of the market. How else might Americans get the message of how buyers and sellers of health care function in markets? Business firms are buying benefits for their employees. They are not terribly altruistic in doing this; rather, they are trying to buy a health care package at the lowest dollar amount. Providers are trying to extract the highest possible revenue for their services, given that they need to discount prices in order to obtain the greatest number of consumers. Even though the buying and selling are done in groups rather than with individuals, the effect of those contracts is similar to open markets.

The effect of managed care on state-determined or -administrated prices (reimbursement rates) through a prospective payment (DRGs, case-mix), the revenue cap system was nothing less than revolutionary. The discounted prices of MCOs were typically lower than those of the DRG system. New York State continued to make "exceptions" for managed care organizations, until the exceptions were to become the rule. On December 31, 1996, the old system—except for Medicare, federal government, and certain state-regulated reimbursement programs, workers' compensation, and no fault—was ended. The New York Health Care Reform Act became effective on January 1, 1997 ("The New York Health Care Reform Act" 1997, pp. 4–5). This act, similar to reform of most states, signaled the "takeover" of managed care in the form of negotiated markets between providers (hospitals, physicians, etc.) and organizations of buyers (business firms and other organizations) on behalf of consumers and/or employees. The market forces prevailed over government-administered prices. In addition, the change indicates that buyers and sellers have choices given the constraints of incomes and prices. There is no one size or type of health care that fits all. On the other hand, we should not feel content given that there are many remaining issues, including the uninsured, quality of care, monopoly or monopsony control, the effective distribution of technology, and the roles of government and markets in maintaining innovative research.

The Issues and Quality Decision Making and Professional Assessment

One of the many issues surrounding MCOs is that of measures of quality, particularly as physicians deem quality to be in their domain. A cartoon shows a medical doctor reporting to his patient in a hospital bed. The physician tells the patient, "You can go home now; the HMO says that you are cured." MCOs have suffered from the wrath of physicians and consumers who want more control of health care. Physicians wanted to be able to make the professional determinations on the type and extent of care and the consequent quality of care. They did not want these decisions made by a registered nurse working for a health maintenance office in a far-off city. Consumers wanted to have more choice and more care under certain circumstances. A mother with a newborn baby may need more than the standard (for HMOs) twenty-four-hour stay in a hospital. More recently, under heavy pressure from consumers, state and federal legislatures and officials amended the stay to forty-eight hours or more. The economist would say, "You want more care? You will have to pay for it." As painful as these constraints may be, any society must be aware of the trade-offs and choices. Also, consumers must be aware that increased benefits of improved health care do come at a cost. Managed care, in an imperfect way, gives us some indication of costs as measured by prices that are determined in these negotiated markets.

There are other issues with managed care. There are concerns about quality of care. James Robinson and Jill Yegian assess the many conflicts within managed care that are getting the attention of economists and policymakers. "Health care companies are under pressure to improve the quality and moderate the costs of health care and yet to refrain from interfering with decision making by physicians and patients" (Robinson and Yegian 2004, on-line pages). This certainly is an issue of quality and how it interfaces with appropriate care. Patients appear to be defining appropriate care "as whatever the informed patient is willing to pay for" (2004, on-line pages). Medical professionals are suggesting that clinical effectiveness should be the criterion for medical decision making. Large employers, public and private, are pressuring insurers to develop disease management and quality improvement programs as criteria for the negotiation of contracts. The background for these initiatives is the extensive research that demonstrates misutilization of medical services when measured against clinical standards. Health care inflation is again rearing its ugly head along with "serious remediable deficiencies in quality of care" (Robinson and Yegian 2004, on-line pages). The health care industry now possesses better predictive ability to allocate scarce medical resources on the most medically needy patients. This adjustment of risk sharing will need either a cooperative health insurance industry or, perhaps, an insurance industry that continues to pool its risks, ignorant of any profits available from avoiding adverse risk selection. Many of the top U.S. health plans now have medical management programs that are designed to moderate costs and manage quality criteria without unnecessarily interfering with decision making by consumers and physicians. This process is accomplished through case studies of disease management. Some health plans emphasize changes in consumer behavior while others emphasize changes in physician behavior. We might think of consumer behavior and physician behavior as the "bookends" of moral hazard. Insured consumers may wish to get as much hospitalization, physician visits, or health care as they or their physicians deem necessary. This moral hazard, along with favorable tax treatment for health insurance, tends to increase demand for health insurance and demand for health care. The inevitable consequence of this demand is higher prices for health care.

Physicians acting as agents for consumers, and as professionals desiring more care rather than best care, could and did exacerbate the demand for health care services. With the development and use of HMOs, moral hazard took a different turn with physicians. HMOs operate on the basis of revenue from subscribers' fees. This revenue, along with some limited nonsubscriber revenues, provides the income under which costs must fall in order for the HMOs to produce profits or surpluses (for the not-for-profit HMOs). Thus, those HMO plans that put limits on expensive hospital stays and favor out-of-hospital services generally are more profitable. The possible moral hazard for physicians is to reduce admissions to hospitals and other expensive resource use. These reductions in services could and have come at the risk of patients. The good news is that this "reversal of economics" may lead to a more efficient allocation of resources. That is, resources are channeled to their most productive and least-cost uses. We should not be anxious to generalize this moral hazard as being typical behavior of HMOs. The other major parties to managed care are the PPOs, which under the umbrella of managed care did have significant effects in lowering the rate of health care inflation. Now there appears to be an attempt at focusing on the appropriate medical or clinical basis for patients, given some insurance caps. Our normative judgment is that health care "ought to be" allocated on a medical need basis and that health insurance should retreat to its original financing role. In Chapter 6, we will be discussing the role of medical savings accounts, which may make the patient a consumer in the sense of selecting the most appropriate type and level of medical care at a price the consumer is able and willing to pay. The combination of high deductible amounts and major medical (or catastrophic) insurance coverage would augur well for a balance between quality care and price/income constraints.

With increasing quality of medical technology and genetic testing, disease management will be viable if it is part of a new vision of public health care policy.

The Report Card for What Have We Wrought: The Cost Savings

David Dranove estimates that by 2005, managed care could produce as much as $301 billion in savings as compared to an absence of managed care. However, he notes that managed care cannot forestall or economize on expenditures on new prescription drugs and technologies. Here the market operates on demand from consumers and the subsequent third-party payers (Dranove 2002, p. 6). There is much evidence to support the thesis that the managed care rate has influenced the rate of increase (adjusted inflation) for per capita expenditures on health care. For five-year intervals, this per capita rate changed significantly from 1985 to 2001. From 1985 to 1990, the rate was 5.8 percent; from 1990 to 1995, the rate was 3.5 percent; and the rate for 1995 to 2000 was 3.1 percent. Managed care is usually credited for this very significant decrease in real per capital spending in the 1990s (U.S. House, Ways and Means 2003, Appendix C, p. C1). However, per capita expenditures for health care increased by 5.1 percent in 2001 with a projected increase of 4.7 percent and 3.6 percent for 2001–2005 and 2005–2010, respectively (U.S. House, Ways and Means 2003, p. C1). We need to consider two factors in any analysis of these numbers. The first factor is the considerable influence of managed care, particularly in light of the major overall increases in health care spending from 1965 to 2001. In the United States total health care spending (in constant 2001 dollars) increased in this period of time from $188.7 billion to $1424.5 billion (U.S. House, Ways and Means 2003, p. C1). This means that there were a number of new services, prescription drugs, and technology developed and used over the thirty-six-year period. We simply had more things to buy. Even so, the rate of increase of spending, per person, continued to experience decreased rates of increase. Second, for part of this time, managed care was "playing second fiddle" to state systems of administered pricing (DRGs, PPS, case-mix determinations). Indeed, to many observers, the fact that MCOs were pricing their services *lower* than those of the state system led to the dismantling of the state systems in favor of today's negotiated markets. The contrast in the effects of prospective payment

Table 4.2

Annual Percentage Change in Selected Components of the Consumer Price Index for All Urban Consumers, 1960–2002 (selected years)

Year	All items	All items less medical care	Medical care total	Physicians' services
1960	1.7	1.3	3.7	2.8
1980	13.5	13.6	11.0	10.5
1986	1.9	1.5	7.5	7.2
1995	2.8	2.7	4.5	4.5
1999	2.2	2.1	3.5	2.8
2002	1.6	1.4	4.7	2.8

Source: U.S. Department of Labor, Bureau of Labor Statistics. Data derived from U.S. House, Ways and Means (2003, Table C-12, p. C20).

systems, including federal DRGs and state case-mix systems, and the effects of MCOs was striking.

In Table 4.2, the consumer price index (CPI) for the medical care component reported an 11.0 percent increase in 1980 and a 7.5 percent increase for 1986. In an approximate sense, these decreases in the rate of increasing prices for health care reflect the effects of the prospective payment system (PPS). This was really an administered price system in which the federal government and most of the states set price (reimbursement) rates. In effect, they said, "Here is your payment for a particular disease category; you need to have a competitive cost structure in order to function in the black." Economies were developed by hospitals. However, the MCOs did better than the PPS-administered pricing schemes through negotiated markets. Eventually, after seeing the decreases in the CPI for medical care of 4.5 percent for 1995 and 3.5 percent for 1999, managed care became the system of choice. By 1997, all but one of the states had dropped the PPS system.

The point is that, in the interim, the relative emphasis on the PPS system had biased the inflation rate; that is, the PPS having rates greater than MCOs caused the rate of spending per person to be higher. Clearly, the market forces were manifest in this reduced rate era. Part of the explanation of the 5.1 percent increase in 2001 is in the reaction against the controls on physician and consumer decision making. We wanted more services and less control; this would cause higher prices, all other things being constant. If we add the major effect of the aging of the population on health care expenditures, we can deduce that without managed care, our rate of increases in spending per person would have been even higher. From 1965 to 2012 (projected), the lowest rise in medical care expenditures was in the late 1990s; this has been attributed to managed care (U.S. House, Ways and Means 2003, p. C7).

Report Card: Utilization

After witnessing major increases in hospital in-patient admissions in the 1970s to a peak of 36 million in 1982 and 1983, the effects of state and federal prospective payment systems became apparent. The decreases continued through the 1980s and up to the trough years of 1994 with 30.7 million admissions (U.S. House, Ways and Means 2003, p. C12). After 1994, the effects of the aging of the population (higher rate of admission and length of stay than people under age sixty-four) and, later, the reaction against managed care became apparent. By 2001, admissions increased to the 1985 level of approximately 33 million. The effect of PPS was to reduce the number of the most costly users of scarce resources, the hospitals. The hospital uses expansive space, registered nurses, medical doctors, and continuing and expensive technology. Alternative out-patient, same-day surgery and less invasive technology combined to reduce admissions and average length of stay for patient. From 1984 to 2001, out-patient visits increased from 212 million to 538 million (U.S. House, Ways and Means 2003, p. C12). There was an attendant increase in emergency room usage to 106 million visits in 2001 from 97 million visits in 1997 (p. C123). This increase was aided by the use of emergency rooms as a last-resort locale for medical care and federal legislation that enabled reimbursement for Medicare and Medicaid patients (2003, p. C13).

Average length of stay is another measure of utilization. Before the introduction of the PPS and MCO as serious policy changes, new less invasive technology and prescription drug use led to a decrease in the average length of stay in hospitals from "over 8 days in the late 1960s to 7.1 in 1982. The implementation of the Medicare PPS system in 1983 caused the average stay to fall further to 6.5 days in 1985 . . . for patients over 64 . . . a decline in length of stay from 10.2 in 1982 to 8.7 in 1985" (U.S. House, Ways and Means 2003, p. C14). The ALOS became a target with the PPS reimbursement. The state versions of PPS were like the federal system in that each DRG or state case-mix category represented a payment cap. Since hospitals know the payment for each category in

advance, they attempted either to reduce costs to take advantage of keeping any profits or surpluses or to "hire" the service out (now called
"outsourcing") to other hospitals. The payments were based, in part, on
length of stay of patients. There were clear incentives for hospitals to
reduce their length of stay.

Anomalies, such as the relative stability of the length of stay in the
late 1980s, were explained by the fact that patients who had longer lengths
of stay became dominant in the mix of all patients. This in itself would
mean that the average length of stay would increase since many of those
with less serious conditions and lower lengths of stay would be treated
as out-patients.

Other utilization and efficiency factors include the supply of hospital
beds and the rates of hospital occupancy. These factors are part of a set
of influences that reflect the major changes in reimbursement. These
changes included the prospective payment system, sometimes referred
to as the federal DRGs or the state case-mix system (1983–97). The
current system of negotiated markets through MCOs has dominated the
current market. The PPS payment scheme, as explained earlier, pres-
sured hospitals to reduce their costs. Consequent changes in number of
hospitals, total beds, and occupancy rates reveal the impact of these
policy changes. These changes are also interrelated with the average
length of stay in hospitals. These are not simply descriptive changes.
Hospitals are the users of the most expensive (scarce) resources, as noted
previously. Even though health care expenditures have increased in the
United States, we are now operating more efficiently; we can enjoy more
health services at a lower cost per unit of service.

Consumers might look past the basic pocketbook measures of increasing expenditures on health services to a more comprehensive view.
We have more services and products of health services and we use them
more intensely. Beginning in 1984, the number of community hospitals
decreased from 5,801 to 4,908 in 2001. The total number of beds for the
same period of time decreased from 1,017,057 to 825,966. As a consequence of fewer hospitals and fewer beds, the occupancy rate *increased*
from 64.3 percent in 1986 to 66.8 percent in 1990. From 1991 to 1996,
the effects of managed care became manifest in the form of lower ALOS.
Even though the number of hospitals and beds decreased through this
period of time, occupancy rates still *decreased* from 66.1 percent to
61.6 percent. From 1986 to 2001, occupancy rates increased as a consequence of further decreases in the number of hospitals (U.S. House,

Ways and Means 2003, p. C15). Also, persons over the age of sixty-five became a more significant proportion of the population and had a larger percentage of hospital admissions and a longer average length of stay. These demographic changes explain the more recent pressures on hospitals for in-patient admissions.

Report Card: Income for Physicians

One of the results of managed care has been to arrange discounts from the listed prices that physicians charge patients for their services. This has been well received by consumers, particularly those using the point-of-service payment system with a co-payment of usually ten dollars. The payment for the service is accomplished without any forms or paperwork on the part of the consumer. The physician is burdened by the extra paperwork for the practice and, of course, by the reduced fee for the services rendered. There are other effects of the changing nature of physician income. A 2001 study by Philip Powell and David Nakata indicated that "financial compensation from physician practice is in decline. After inflation, physician net income (after expenses, before taxes) per hour of patient care fell 3.1 percent between 1993 and 1997. During this same 5-year period, real hourly net income across a sample of less general medical specialties (anesthesia, obstetrics/gynecology, radiology, surgery) experienced a more dramatic fall of 10.7 percent" (2001, pp. 360–361). Powell and Nakata attributed much of this decline to managed care contracts as well as the effects of the Resource-based Relative Value Scale (RBRVS) physician reimbursement system under Medicare. For many years, the RBRVS scheme has restricted payments to physicians. Competition from foreign doctors, nurse practitioners, physician's assistants, and midwives has increased and allowed some substitution for some of the services of physicians. Also, the attempts of physicians to respond to managed care in the form of collective bargaining have not been very successful. Combined with the loss of market power and decision making under managed care is the current and potential decrease in physician earnings. This set of perceived threats has been sufficient for physicians to consider early retirement.

The advent of Buyers' Clubs has produced some sovereignty for consumers as well as bargaining power. When people have to pay out-of-pocket expenses, the dynamics of the market come into play. Out-of-pocket payment is quick, easy, and less expensive for the physi-

Table 4.3

Percentage of Total Physician Expenditures (selected years)

Source of funding	1965	1980	1995	2000	2001
Out-of-pocket	58.5	30.2	11.9	11.6	11.2
Third-party	41.5	69.8	88.1	88.4	88.8
Private health insurance	33.0	35.3	48.6	47.6	48.1
Other private	1.5	3.9	8.0	7.5	7.1
Government	6.9	30.5	31.5	33.3	33.6
Federal	1.6	24.1	25.5	27.6	27.7
Medicare	0.0	17.4	18.9	20.6	20.4
Medicaid (incl. SCHIP expansion)[1]	0.0	2.9	3.9	3.9	4.0
Other federal	1.6	3.7	2.7	3.1	3.3
State and local	5.3	6.6	6.0	5.7	5.9
Medicaid (incl. SCHIP expansion)[2]	0.0	2.3	2.8	2.7	2.9
Other state and local	5.3	4.2	3.3	3.0	3.0

Source: Centers for Medicare and Medicaid Services, Office of the Actuary. Percentages calculated by Congressional Research Service.
Derived from data in U.S. House, Ways and Means (2003 Table C-11, p. C9).
[1]Federal share only.
[2]State and local share only.
SCHIP = State Child Health Insurance Program.

cian in terms of billings, office personnel, and insurance forms. At the margin, the physician may be willing to accept $1,400 for a sticker price of $2,400 for a medical procedure. At that moment the price paid by the consumer, which is the price accepted by the provider, represents the marginal value to both parties. This is atypical in managed care, with bargaining for the two parties accomplished by a third party representing groups. An important possible consequence of the decline in hourly income for physicians is the loss of specialists in key areas when early retirement becomes a viable option.

Payment for physicians' services is heavily influenced by third-party payments, accounting for 88.8 percent of the total payments in 2001. Private health insurance payments to physicians increased to 48.6 percent in 1995 as compared to 33 percent in 1965. The private insurance payments remained relatively constant for the period of 1996–2001 at about 48 percent. As one might expect, during the years of increases in private insurance coverage, the out-of-pocket percentage of all physician revenue *decreased* from 58.5 percent in 1965 to 11.2 percent in 2001([see Table 4.3] (U.S. House, Ways and Means 2003, pp. C17, C18).

Much of the pattern seen in Table 4.3 can be attributed to the rise of managed care. We might expect some reversal in these patterns if medical savings accounts (MSAs) and health savings accounts (HSAs) become more widely used. These accounts allow consumers to shop for some medical services, including those of physicians. This would translate into more out-of-pocket expenditures as opposed to private insurance payments. This projected trend is compounded by the decreased share of employees' health care benefits borne by the employer. From 1983 to 1998, the employer share of health care costs decreased from 45.5 percent to 26.6 percent. The out-of-pocket medical spending (in constant 1998 dollars) was up to $199.5 billion in 1998 from $144.6 billion in 1990, an increase of 38 percent. Not all of this out-of-pocket spending is for conventional medical care. Alternative medical care, such as acupuncture, amounted to $30 billion a year in 1998. Even people covered by insurance were shopping on-line for additional coverage. Buyers' Clubs and individually brokered services are providing both discounted prices and more coverage than the usual array of insurance or third-party systems (Freudenheim 2000, pp. A1 and C19).

In 2000, 40.8 percent of physician income was attributable to managed care contracts. The percentage of income derived from managed care varied among specialties, with OB/GYN at 56.4 percent and psychiatry at 28.6 percent (U.S. House, Ways and Means 2003, p. C18). We may experience some decline in these numbers as dissatisfaction with managed care turns consumers into individuals shopping in the marketplace as described earlier.

Report Card: Managed Care—Consolidation and Competition

In the environment of rapid and widespread consolidations of hospitals, many issues are of concern. Do these consolidations cause hospital prices to increase? Do for-profit hospital consolidations lead to higher prices than not-for-profit consolidations? Do the results differ on the degree of market power? How have managed care contracts affected the outcomes?

In a review of these questions, Glenn Melnick, Emmett Keeler, and Jack Zwanziger (1999) produce empirical results on reduced competition from hospital mergers. Price increases tend to occur for the merged hospitals and the remaining hospitals. The increase in hospital mergers and acquisitions increased from 100 in 1994 to 184 in 1997. The 1997 arrangements included 290 hospitals and over 47,000 beds. Much of this merger action was a response to the collective power of managed care (p. 167). Hospitals can more effectively bargain with managed care organizations if they have greater market power in the form of one voice. This can be called a countervailing force on the part of providers of health care services.

Over 75 percent of all of the mergers and acquisitions in 1997 involved not-for-profit hospitals. This has put managed care in an unusual position of trying to negotiate lower prices from hospitals. However, not-for-profit hospitals will be able to exploit their new merged power to use monopoly pricing power in areas where competition has been weakened. This will mean that not-for-profit hospitals will need to become market competitors despite their lack of a full commitment to profit maximizing (Melnick, Keeler, and Zwanziger 1999, pp. 167–169). Market power or share of market, as opposed to for-profit or not-for-profit status, has the more significant effect. That is, the greater the share of market, the greater the upward pressures on prices. However, the for-profits are more affected by the increased concentration of hospitals. They tend to be more motivated by profits. All other factors constant, price increases for merged for-profit hospitals are in the 40 percent range while the price increases tend to be in the 25 percent range. So, both ownership and market share play roles in the degrees of price increases (Melnick, Keeler, and Zwanziger 1999, pp. 168–169).

Some of the preceding cases can result in positive gains for consumers with efficiency gains from consolidation of hospitals. These savings could also be confiscated by hospital market power, which would allow hospitals to raise prices in negotiated markets. A more recent study by Capps and Dranove found that consolidations increased prices in three of the four markets studied (Capps and Dranove 2004, pp. 175–177). To examine the effects of managed care, these researchers used PPO contracts as a proxy for all managed care contracts, including HMOs. Since the contracts varied widely, Capps and Dranove used the most popular PPO contract as its proxy for all PPOs. The results verified the expectation of increases in prices (Capps and Dranove 2004, pp. 178–180).

Many observers of hospital pricing behavior after mergers feel that more effective anti-trust action by the Federal Trade Commission (FTC) and/or the anti-trust division of the Department of Justice is in order. Even though these agencies did take successful action to block consolidations of hospitals in the 1980s and early 1990s and then lost five cases later in the 1990s, they have not initiated any action on hospital consolidations since 1998 (Capps and Dranove 2004, p. 175). A leading scholar in this field, Deborah Haas-Wilson, feels that there needs to be a relatively strong emphasis on anti-trust action as opposed to regulation, per se: "Given the increasing reliance on markets to allocate health care resources, to constrain health care costs, and to promote both low health care prices and high health care quality, it is essential that policy makers seek to ensure that these markets work well" (Haas-Wilson 2003, p. 9). It may come as a surprise to some that conservative economists, such as Milton Friedman, believe strongly in anti-trust action. If markets are to remain viable and effective, they *must* be competitive. Otherwise, the effort to provide low costs as an incentive to produce and to provide low prices for consumers will be in serious jeopardy. However important anti-trust law may be for hospital pricing issues, its application to some other health care areas is limited by law. The McCarron-Ferguson Act exempts "the business of insurance or activities that involve spreading or transferring risk or that implicate relationships between policy holders and insurers, from the federal anti-trust laws" (Haas-Wilson 2003, p. 80).

Report Card: Technology and Managed Care

Burton Weisbrod (1991) and, in 1998, Michael E. Chernew and colleagues wrote review articles on the relationships among insurance, technology, and costs. Weisbrod explored how increased use of insurance could affect the development of technology. Conversely, increases in medical technology could influence the extent and use of the insurance necessary to finance any expansion of medical technology. Given the extensive use of subsidies for insurance, its increased use tends to increase the demand for health care and leads to a subsequent rise in the costs of acquiring health care. Weisbrod considered both the amount and type of insurance in these complex relationships. The change in the nature of insurance from that which was based on a retrospective determination of costs incurred by the hospital for particular patients, to a prospective system that determines prices/costs (reimbursement) that were largely independent of costs incurred on behalf of any particular patient, represented a major change (Weisbrod 1991, p. 528). This change was, at first, mostly in the form of the prospective payment system with the diagnostic related groups of Medicare and similar case-mix code systems in the states, as identified earlier in this chapter. Except for Medicare, managed care organizations became the dominant form in the 1990s. Even though Weisbrod's article was published in 1991, he clearly identified HMOs as a new force in insurance and in medical care pricing.

These major changes in the insurance system "altered incentives to use existing health care resources (that is, their rate of diffusion and utilization) and altered incentives for the R&D sector to invest in developing medical care techniques that were of higher quality but more costly" (Weisbrod 1991, p. 528). Again, we begin to see the cost of providing services being separately determined from the administered price (by DRG code) of a government agency. Nevertheless, a powerful change in resource allocation and incentives for new technology was born. The expansion of insurance aids and abets the new medical technologies.

In the Chernew (1998) article, the scope of the inquiry about technology and costs is expanded to focus on the effects of managed care on health care expenditures and on the related matter of medical technology. Chernew and colleagues define medical technology as "the application of 'some technology' to a health care problem" (Chernew et al. 1998, p. 261). This general definition would, in the simplest sense, include all health care services since they all have applied some early methods of technology broadly defined. Weisbrod, in his 1991 review article, takes a similar approach to the definition of technology. He talks about new technologies as "any new knowledge about health care" (Weisbrod 1991, p. 524) and "advances in medical technology—involving both diagnostics and treatment" (p. 530). Chernew et al. believe that we need some distinctions in the overall definition of technology in order to properly assess the "relationship between medical technology and cost growth" (p. 261). Chernew and his co-authors define *new* medical technology as "new knowledge regarding the delivery of new services . . . that has the potential to change physician practice and influence health care cost growth" (pp. 261–262). This definition would include new ways and new technology for delivery of health care. The diffusion of new technology might take place over a number of years, as recognized by both Chernew and Weisbrod. This is important in analyzing both the cost-effectiveness of technological change in connecting new technology and its contribution to changes in cost. New technology might represent cost savings that include the substitution of the new technology for an older one. Less invasive surgical techniques usually represent substitution for an older method;

for example, laser surgery for gall bladder removal can take place on a same-day surgery basis while the old, more invasive method would require a stay of six or seven days or more. The per-day charge can be more expensive for the new method but the total cost of the illness will be considerably lower than for the old method.

We have thus experienced a major reduction in needed use of expensive hospital resources. Also, the patient returns to home or work more quickly. The opportunity costs of surgery decrease appreciably. However, there may be complementary costs that increase. The costs of research, development, and training of personnel may increase health care expenditures. Chernew and co-authors review the literature on the effects of managed care on cost growth. The "horse race" approach simply compares HMOs or strongly managed plans with fee-for-service (FFS) or less managed plans. For the plans reviewed, the ratio of HMO cost growth to FSS cost growth per year studied were 95.8 percent, 98.9 percent, 96.0 percent, and 80.4 percent. The last two percentages were from the data for the years 1991–1995 using different data sets. The first two percentages were derived from data for the years 1962/1963–1970/1971 and for the years 1976–1981, respectively (Chernew et al. 1998, pp. 266–267). The "market comparison" approach to studies was also reviewed by Chernew. This approach compares cost growth in distinctively different markets that differ in the degree of penetration of managed care organizations. Over twelve studies of these market comparison studies were reviewed. The studies generally supported the contention that managed care had a competitive effect on health care costs. For example, a study by Gaskin and Hadley in 1997 found "hospital cost growth to be inversely related to HMO penetration" (Chernew et al. 1998, pp. 268–273). Some of the effects of managed care on reducing hospital cost growth reached beyond the MCO network. In some cases, the outcomes of negotiated markets between buyers and sellers of services inside the MCO network set new standards for buyers and sellers outside the MCO. These new standards of practice would include the use of economizing measures such as alternatives to expensive hospitalizations and lower lengths of stay. With respect to the relationship of medical technology and its diffusion to cost growth, Chernew feels that empirical studies support the premise that "inflation stems from increases in costs due to the development and diffusion of medical technology induced by high levels of insurance coverage" (Chernew et al. 1998, p. 276).

Managed Care: What Have We Learned? The Policy Implications

Some call it a revolution; others call it an evolution or a devolution. Revolution is defined as a complex change or "a round of successive changes or events of a radical and usually sudden change of government, or of character, social conditions or the like." Evolution is "a process in which something complex is developed from simple beginnings." Devolution is the act of "delivering to another; a passing to a successor" (all definitions are from Funk and Wagnall's *Desk Standard Dictionary, Ready Reference Edition*).

Each of these terms could fit as a description of the changes in our health care system. Each term could carry a policy implication. However, their collective impact does suggest an interrelationship among the terms. In many ways, we could justify a "revolution" in health care policy. The market for health care is more than simply a place for buyer and seller to meet. Negotiated markets have allowed managed care organizations to demonstrate how price mechanisms can trump government-administrated prices. This is a revolution in policy and has the possibility of finding a role for markets that is competitive with government oversight. There seems to be a policy lesson here. Are we willing to use competition and market forces to test their ability to tame inflation and to allow consumers some shopping for individual "baskets" of health care services that suit individual needs and pocketbooks? We have gained some insights on how to "manage" diseases guided by genetic information. Can professionals tell us our individual "healthprints" and guide us to individually and clinically designed programs of care? If so, it is becoming more apparent that we need some market baskets to match our health needs. We have some tests coming up. The Medicare reforms beginning in 2004 and continuing in full force in 2006 for pharmaceutical products will test the ability of competitive market forces under a government-designed system. Even given the number of medically uninsured, the viability of a single-payer system or universal health care system is questionable.

Evolution of a complex ending from a humble beginning seems to fit the theme of this chapter. Health insurance first appeared in the 1950s, and through the early 1960s it was mostly a method of financing rather than directing health care decisions. For a period of time we had some government direction of health care, particularly with reimbursement rates for hospitals. The complexity came when the government agencies competed with managed care organizations to foster discounted health care prices. Government lost the battle, but the complexities have continued in finding a market/government balance.

Devolution has taken place and is used in the current health care literature. Devolution describes the degree to which a nation passes some of the federal or national authority to a regional or local government or even to a private authority. The United Kingdom has authorized funds for physicians and hospitals to do their own shopping for greater internal efficiency even under a nationalized health system. Medical savings accounts allow a devolution of spending decisions from government or insurance to consumers. More about all of this in the ensuing chapters.

5

The Four "Cs" of the Uninsured

Causes, Characteristics, Consequences, and Corrections/Choices

The Setting

Increasing health care costs, reduced amounts of employment-based health care insurance coverage, and changes in the composition of the labor force have combined to make access to health care insurance, and hence, health care more difficult. It would be tempting to make this a short story and simply say that all of the above are the basis for the over 43 million Americans without health insurance in 2002 (U.S. House, Ways and Means 2003, p. C34). However, there have been a number of positive changes in the 1990s. These changes include the decline of national health expenditures "as a share of national income for the longest period since the Great Depression. . . . While per capita costs had grown at an inflation-adjusted rate of 4.7 percent between 1950 and 1993, they grew at . . . less than 1.9 percent between 1993 and 1999. By 1999, health care spending was 25 percent lower than might have been expected based on historic growth rates" (Glied 2003, p. 125). During this period of time, the United States benefited from lower-than-expected rates of increase in Medicare and Medicaid spending. The states received new matching federal funds via the State Child Health Insurance Program (SCHIP). This allowed almost 30 million children to have health insurance coverage. By 2000, the uninsured as a percentage of Americans fell (Glied 2003, p. 125). Mark Pauly feels that medical insurance has improved significantly since the 1960s. The coverage is "more widespread, and private insurance covers a much larger fraction of total spending . . . managed care insurance has greatly reduced the risk of unexpected financial payment . . . [and has provided] the generation of more informative prices and quality measures" (Pauly 2001, p. 833). However, since 2000, increasing health care costs have driven insurance premiums higher. This reversal to higher costs can, in part, be explained by anti-competitive forces including mergers and acquisitions in managed care organizations (MCOs). Also, there has been control of some local markets by for-profit hospitals (see Chapter 4, on managed care). Moreover, consumer and provider pressure for more coverage and decision making in MCOs has led to more services, albeit at higher prices.

There are some anomalies in health insurance. As consumers receive more insurance coverage as a result of tax incentives for both employers and employees, the demand for health care increases. As the demand for health care increases, ceteris paribus, the prices for health care increase. These changes will likely have adverse effects on the low-income population and the uninsured. Their access to health care would be lessened. Even as MCOs negotiate lower prices from health care providers, those outside of these contracts face higher prices. As discussed in Chapter 4, on managed care, the discounted prices are only for those who participate as enrollees in these plans. Indeed, the uninsured often face higher prices for the same medical care received by MCO enrollees. This should be obvious. The MCO wants to negotiate lower prices for its enrolled population. If the same discounted prices were available for nonmembers, why would anyone join the MCO? It is the "free rider" problem that labor unions face in open shops for collective bargaining. Thus, my lower price as an enrollee in an MCO does not lower the price for the uninsured nor does it raise the price, except in a relative sense. The significant policy issue is that there is an exclusion characteristic. That is, those who do not enroll in an HMO are excluded from its benefits. Another anomaly of health insurance is that it can often, if not always, increase costs of health insurance. For example, if everyone had complete health insurance coverage for up to two visits a year for a physical exam with a primary care physician, the cost increase would be greater than that represented by the cost per visit times the number of visits. The handling of the insurance forms would increase the costs. Also, we would likely have a greater number of visits than would have occurred with less coverage. There would be externalities or secondary effects of more care for primary visits than medically necessary, causing less of other medical services. Also, we would have fewer scarce resources to provide other public and private goods and services.

As long as we have some functioning of private markets in health care and health insurance, there are some fundamental issues. These issues become the subject matter of applied economies in policy decisions. Insurance is all about risk at some price or premium. The premium is designed to reflect the actuarial risk, administrative cost, and profit or surplus (not-for-profit) for the insurance carriers. The uncertainty about future health care costs, the desire to reduce the risks, and the subsidization of health insurance by government and business firms tend to "shelter consumers of medical services from many of the financial consequences of their decisions. This separation between the price paid by patients and the total cost of the services they use leads to moral hazard" (Glied 2003, p. 126). This moral hazard is the overuse of medical services by the insured since the consumer does not experience any out-of-pocket expense at the time the service is rendered. This opens up an opportunity for using deductibles and/or co-payments as rationing devices to solicit economizing by consumers in health care decisions. The more the consumer has to pay "up front" in the form of a deductible, as in automobile insurance, the fewer the claims to be underwritten by the insurance company, an MCO, an employer, or the government. The Medicare patient has to pay around $900 before the government takes over hospital payment, with some restrictions and co-payments. Most MCOs require a co-payment for physician services, hospital stays, and pharmaceutical drugs. As we will see in Chapter 7, on Medicare reform, co-payments are part of the new pharmaceutical benefits program enacted in 2003. There are many policy implications in deductibles and co-payments. The use of deductibles allows cooperative arrangements with government and business. For example, medical savings accounts (MSAs) and health savings accounts (HSAs) combine large deductibles with major medical insurance policies. These function on the basis of relatively low premiums as well as consumer choice in shopping for health care to reduce health care costs. The positive policy implications include the major cost savings from cost sharing.

Rexford Santerre and Stephen Neun report on a number of studies that analyze the effects of co-insurance (deductibles, co-payments) on the demand for health insurance. These studies include the Rand Health Insurance Study (RAND HIS) in which "it is apparent that if either the rate of coinsurance or the deductible falls, the amount of health care consumed increases" (Santerre and Neun 2000, p. 114). These studies and others suggest implicitly that there is a role for private insurance in reducing the costs of moral hazard. Santerre and Neun, on the basis of empirical studies, suggest that "in the absence of the tax subsidy on employer-provided health benefits, competition creates incentives for insurers to minimize the total overhead costs" (Santerre and Neun 2000, p. 403). Beyond all of this, we still do have a major problem with approximately 43 million Americans without health insurance. This number may be biased in both directions. An upward bias might reflect the fact that "many uninsured people choose to be without health insurance and because the spell without insurance is relatively short" (Santerre and Neun 2000, p. 406). Downward biases might reflect job security in jobs that provide either little or no health insurance. Some of these jobs might offer other benefits or location that would make it difficult for workers to leave. In the quest for greater efficiency, some firms might put equity issues on hold. Considerations of equity, efficiency costs, public goods, private markets, and a role for government will all have markers in policy choices. We will return to policy issues at the end of this chapter.

This chapter explores the status of the medically uninsured in terms of their numbers, percentage of population, demographic composition, employment characteristics, income, age, race, poverty level, citizenship, and out-of-pocket expenses. Data on these points will give us some clues as to the causes of being uninsured to determine which factors allow a discretionary role for policy changes or suggestions. An identification and measure of the social and private consequences of the uninsured will be followed by an examination of corrections, modifications, and new remedies for any institutional, market, or government actions.

The Uninsured: Who Are They?

The Characteristics

The major categories for characterizing the uninsured population are age, race/ethnicity, employment, income, and poverty status. With respect to age, we can exclude the over-sixty-five population from this analysis since 95 percent were covered under the federal program of Medicare. Less than 1 percent of the over-sixty-five group were without insurance for the whole year of 2002 (U.S. House, Ways and Means 2003, p. C34).

For the age groups under the age of sixty-five, there are significant differences in health insurance coverage (see Figure 5.1). There is a "saucer" distribution, with the lowest percentage of the uninsured at the two ends of the age spectrum. For the population under the age of five, about 5 percent were without insurance. For the population between ages fifty-

Figure 5.1   **Characteristics of the Uninsured Population Under Age 65, 2002** (age and race/ethnicity)

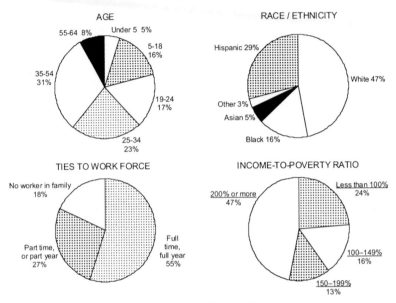

Source: U.S. House, Ways and Means (2003, p. C42).

five and sixty-four, about 8 percent were medically uninsured. Medicaid, the State Children's Health Insurance Program (SCHIP), and other subsidized programs have had strong positive effects on access to health insurance (U.S. House, Ways and Means 2003, p. C34). From 1996–1999, there was a decrease from about 10 percent to just under 8 percent for children who were uninsured all year (Rhoades, Cohen, and Vistnes 2003, p. 1). For the age group eighteen to twenty-four years of age, over 22 percent lacked health insurance for a full year while over 45 percent did not have insurance at some point during the year (Rhoades 2003, p. 5). However, the statistics in Figure 5.1 appear to tell a different story. These statistics report the percentage of all of the age groups represented by a particular age group. The numbers in each pie graph must total 100 percent. For the age group nineteen to twenty-four, the 17 percent figure represents their share of all age groups. The Medical Expenditure Panel Survey (MEPS) figure of over 22 percent represents the percentage of all people in the eighteen to twenty-four age group that were unemployed for a full year (Rhoades 2003, p. 5). This post-pediatric age group is the healthiest in the United States and often decides to remain without insurance. Some are covered with insurance during their undergraduate study years. Excluding the over-sixty-five age group, the percentage of two of the three remaining age groups without insurance increases as compared to the nineteen to twenty-four age group. In 2002, the twenty-five to thirty-four age group had a 23 percent share of the uninsured; the thirty-five to fifty-four age group had a 31 percent share. The age group of fifty-five to sixty-four represented only 8 percent of the medically uninsured (see Figure 5.1; U.S. House, Ways and Means 2003, pp. C34 and C41).

The race/ethnicity characteristic is a clear example of a needed two-way analysis of the data. There are clear differences between the percentage of all uninsured for a particular ethnic group and the percentage of the population of the same ethnic group that is uninsured. For example, Figure 5.1 shows that whites are 47 percent of all of the uninsured for 2002. It also shows that Hispanics are 29 percent and that blacks are 16 percent of the uninsured. However, in Table 5.1, uninsured whites are over 12 percent of the white population, uninsured Hispanics are 34 percent of the Hispanic population, and uninsured blacks are over 21 percent of the black population. Both views are important, particularly for policy prescriptions (all of the figures in Figure 5.1 and Table 5.1 are for the uninsured under the age of sixty-five).

Much of the concern about the uninsured is related to employment status (see Table 5.2). It would seem intuitively obvious that the lack of medical insurance is tied to the lack of employment. However, 82 percent of the medically uninsured either worked full-time for a full year (55 percent) or part-time or part of a year (27 percent) in 2002 (U.S. House, Ways and Means 2003, pp. C39–C41). So, we need to look more closely at the type of work and the size of the employing firm. The type of work is also a major determinant of insurance coverage. Many of the jobs in the services sector, particularly in entertainment, lodging, food, and the arts, have great variability in duration of work and are likely to have high levels of uninsurance. In these specific areas, 34 percent were without insurance for 2002 (U.S. House, Ways and Means 2003, p. C39). Some of these workers have more than one employer. An actor or actress may wait tables and also act in a performance or audition for a role. Many of fast-food workers are teenagers and work part-time; often these employees are not insured by their employees because of their temporary status. Some of these young workers are insured by their parents' or school policies. We have heard about "starving artists"; we can often add the term "uninsured artists." We can also identify other characteris-

Table 5.1

Health Insurance Coverage by Type of Insurance and Demographic Characteristics for People Under Age 65, 2002

| | Population (in millions) | Type of insurance[1] | | | Uninsured | |
		Employ-ment based[2]	Public[2]	Other[4]	Percent	Millions
Race/ethnicity:						
White	166.4	73.4	9.4	10.8	12.4	20.7
Black	31.7	54.0	25.3	6.9	21.5	6.8
Hispanic	37.3	44.5	20.8	5.1	34.0	12.7
Asian	10.4	64.3	9.7	11.7	19.7	2.1
Other	5.8	58.4	21.6	11.0	18.4	1.1
Family type:						
Two parents	112.7	74.0	10.5	9.6	12.6	14.2
Single dad with children	7.3	50.5	20.8	6.7	28.0	2.0
Single mom with children	30.4	44.8	37.1	4.8	20.1	6.1
No children	101.3	65.8	8.9	10.9	20.7	20.9
Region:						
Northeast	46.8	69.7	13.8	6.6	15.0	7.0
Midwest	57.0	73.0	11.8	8.1	13.2	7.5
South	89.3	63.1	13.9	10.8	19.8	17.7
West	58.6	62.9	13.8	11.2	19.0	11.2
Income-to-poverty ratio:[5]						
Less than 100	31.0	20.0	44.3	7.3	33.6	10.4
100–149	21.6	35.7	30.5	8.6	32.2	7.0
150–199	21.2	52.4	19.5	8.5	26.8	5.7
200+	177.2	80.3	5.1	10.1	11.3	20.0
Citizenship						
Native	221.9	68.8	13.8	9.8	14.5	32.3
Naturalized	10.3	64.4	9.2	9.5	21.6	2.2
Noncitizen	19.5	41.5	10.4	5.9	45.3	8.8
Total	251.7	66.5	13.4	9.5	17.2	43.3

Sources: Congressional Research Service analysis of data from the March 2003 Current Population Survey; U.S. House, Ways and Means (2003, p. C36).

[1]People may have more than one source of coverage; percentages may total to more than 100.

[2]Group health insurance through current or former employer or union. Excludes military and veterans' coverage.

[3]Includes Medicare, Medicaid, the State Children's Health Insurance Program (SCHIP), and other state programs for low-income individuals. Excludes military and veterans' coverage.

[4]Private nongroup health insurance, military or veterans' coverage.

[5]In 2002, the poverty threshold for a family of four with two children was $18,244. Approximately 616,000 children are excluded from CPS-based poverty analyses because they are living with a family to which they are unrelated. These are usually foster children.

Figure 5.2 **Characteristics of the Uninsured Population Under Age 65, 2002** (citizenship and firm size)

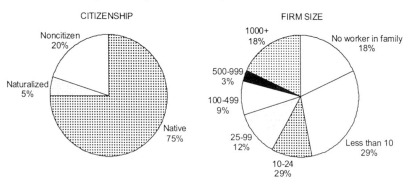

Source: Congressional Research Service analysis of data from March 2003 Current Population Survey; U.S. House, Ways and Means (2003, p. C42).

Note: Totals may not sum to 100 percent due to rounding. Hispanics may be of any race. In this chart, whites, blacks, and Asians are those who are non-Hispanics and report only one race. Among non-Hispanics, individuals who report any other single race (e.g., American Indian) or multiple races are categorized as "other." "Firm size" and "ties to work force" reflect the employment characteristics of the primary worker in families where someone is working. Those characteristics were applied to those individuals' "dependents"—their spouses and children. Employed policyholders of private coverage are first to be assigned as primary workers. For those in families without private coverage, persons' employment characteristics are those of the family head or, if the head is not employed and the spouse is, the spouse.

tics of employment that have an interrelationship with the type of work. Workers in firms with fewer than ten employees accounted for 29 percent of the uninsured in 2002. For the same year, workers in firms with over 1,000 employees accounted for 18 percent of the uninsured (U.S. House, Ways and Means 2003, pp. C39, C42). See Figure 5.2 for further details.

If we combine some of these characteristics, we begin to get a clearer profile of the uninsured. The following group characteristics are over-represented among the uninsured (that is, a higher portion of the uninsured than their proportion of the population): young adults, full-time/full-year workers, Hispanics, and people with incomes below the poverty level.

The plight of the uninsured relates in many ways to the continuing issue of public versus private coverage. This issue is also related to access to health care and who pays for any resolution of this gap in our health care system. This problem is complicated by the changing nature

Table 5.2

Health Insurance Coverage by Employment Characteristics[1] for People Under Age 65, 2002

	Population (millions)	Type of Insurance[2]			Uninsured	
		From own job[3]	From others' job[3]	Other[4]	Percent	Millions
People in families with a worker[5]	216.5	36.2	38.0	18.2	16.3	35.3
Firm size[1,5]						
Under 10	37.0	19.7	20.4	31.1	34.3	12.7
10–24	18.5	30.2	28.8	21.3	26.0	4.8
25–99	27.4	36.9	35.4	17.6	18.5	5.1
100–499	31.0	40.8	42.4	14.1	11.9	3.7
500–999	12.6	42.3	45.7	12.3	9.4	1.2
1,000+	90.1	41.6	45.3	14.7	8.8	7.9
Industry[1,5]						
Arts, entertainment, recreation, food services, accommodation	14.4	26.3	20.5	25.2	33.7	4.9
Agriculture, forestry, fishing, and hunting	3.2	19.2	23.6	32.7	30.9	1.0
Other services	8.9	26.4	24.5	26.5	29.4	2.6
Construction	18.4	25.9	31.8	19.3	29.0	5.3
Wholesale, retail trade	29.1	35.9	34.6	19.6	18.3	5.3
Professional, management, administrative services	21.6	35.3	36.1	18.7	18.2	3.9
Transportation, utilities	13.0	36.7	44.3	14.1	13.5	1.7
Manufacturing	32.0	38.9	45.8	11.8	11.3	3.6
Educational, health, and social services	40.5	42.6	40.1	17.6	10.5	4.2
Mining	1.3	35.7	51.4	13.9	9.5	0.1
Finance, insurance, real estate, rental and leasing	15.4	39.9	44.7	14.7	9.4	1.4
Information	6.4	42.4	44.2	12.8	9.0	0.6
Public administration	10.5	45.9	48.5	11.8	5.1	0.5
Armed forces, military	1.8	16.0	28.8	100.0	0.0	0.0

Labor force attachment[1,5]						
Full-time, full year	171.7	38.2	41.5	15.0	13.8	23.7
Full-time, part year	25.6	32.2	27.8	27.1	23.8	6.1
Part-time, full year	11.1	26.8	23.3	30.4	27.4	3.0
Part-time, part year	8.2	20.9	16.5	41.2	30.2	2.5
People in families without a worker[5]	28.0	13.8[6]	9.6	54.6	28.5	8.0
People with coverage outside the home	7.2	7.7	100.0	17.1	0.0	0.0
Total	251.7	32.9	36.6	22.2	17.2	43.3

Sources: Congressional Research Service analysis of data from the March 2003 Current Population Survey; U.S. House, Ways and Means (2003, pp. C37, C38).

[1]The employment characteristics are those of the policyholder. In families without private coverage, "workers" are the family head or, if the head is not employed, the spouse. For "dependents," the employment characteristics are those of the person providing dependent coverage or, if the dependent has no private health insurance, of the head of household or spouse.

[2]People may have more than one source of health insurance during the year; therefore percentages may total more than 100.

[3]Group health insurance through current or former employer or union.

[4]Medicare, Medicaid, SCHIP, and other government coverage, nongroup health insurance, and military and veterans' coverage.

[5]For persons who worked and their dependents and who did not receive private coverage through a person not in the household.

[6]Nearly 90 percent of these policyholders (i.e., those who did not work during the year but had employment-based coverage in their name) were retirees, were ill or disabled, or were at home with the family and probably received coverage through their former employer.

of public and private coverage. In the United States, government insurance through Medicare and Medicaid increased its coverage of the population from 1987 to 1993 and from 1999 to 2002. This increase took place at the same time that there were declines in the percentage of the population with employment-based coverage (U.S. House, Ways and Means 2003, p. C40). These opposite directions of the business firms and the government were in some ways related. As more employees lost coverage through job loss, outsourcing, more sharing of insurance costs, retirement, or moving from full-time to part-time work, they became eligible for government-sponsored insurance such as Medicaid or Medicare. Some of the reversal of these trends was apparent during periods of economic growth such as the mid to late 1990s, when employment-based coverage increased.

Much of the more recent increase in government financing of health insurance has come through the increasing use of Medicaid and its explosive increases in costs, and through the State Children's Health Insurance Program (SCHIP). Indeed, the decline in the number of children without insurance from 1996 to 1999 was attributable to both public and private insurance programs. During this period of time, the number of children covered by private insurance increased from 39.8 million to 41.2 million. The increase in the number of children covered by public insurance increased from 11.4 million to 12.4 million (Rhoades et al. 2003, pp. 6–7).

The type of work, the size of the firm, and the availability of private insurance or public insurance are important factors in determining the probability of being uninsured. The hourly wage is also significant. In 2000, workers earning less than ten dollars an hour were ten times as likely to be medically uninsured as workers earning twenty dollars or more an hour. For the same year, low wage earners represented about one-third of all wage earners, yet comprised two-thirds of the total number of the uninsured.

The ratio of income to poverty provides clues to the probability of being uninsured. In 2002, 11 percent of people whose incomes were at least twice that of the poverty level lacked health insurance. This compares to 34 percent of people with incomes below the poverty line who were uninsured. The ratio of employer-based to publicly financed insurance varied directly with the income-to-poverty ratio. That is, "eighty percent of people with incomes at least two times the poverty level were covered through an employer, and only 5 percent had public coverage"

(U.S. House, Ways and Means 2003, p. C39). The ratio for those below the poverty line was different. Twenty percent of these people were covered by an employer-based plan, with 44 percent receiving publicly financed insurance (U.S. House, Ways and Means 2003, pp. C39, C41, Chart C-2; also see Figure 5.1).

The Causes

Many of the causes of people being uninsured can be gleaned by identifying their characteristics. For any analysis, we need to determine whether the characteristics are causal, associated, or independent of the status or changes in the numbers of the uninsured. Also, we need to know if the causal factors are discretionary or nondiscretionary for any desired policy change. For example, young people require less insurance than older people because their age group is healthier than the older group. Should we adopt a government policy to limit the number of older people who are permitted to have insurance? Of course, this is absurd. It only illustrates a nondiscretionary variable. Once we determine the major factors that explain changes (causal) in the number of the uninsured, we can make policy suggestions accordingly. For example, if the lack of insurance is coupled with higher prices for the uninsured, we explain the unique predicament of the uninsured. They lack financial access to the system with no insurance, insufficient income, and having to pay higher prices than the insured. Two of these conditions lend themselves to discretionary policy choices. They are the lack of insurance and the higher prices. Insufficient income is part of a set of adverse conditions for the poor and is not subject to immediate discretionary action.

Much of this dilemma can be explained by the unique pricing systems of most hospitals in the United States. Part of this pricing system is common to other industries. We know that few people pay the list or manufacturer's suggested retail price on automobiles or a number of other goods. So, we have list prices and we have transaction prices. In the health care industry, particularly for hospitals, we have the distinction between charges (presumably based on costs) and transaction or discounted prices. In Chapter 4, on managed care, the history of institutional pricing is reviewed. Suffice it to say that we have entered an era of market forces that have allowed managed care companies and others to negotiate discounted prices for their clients. These are negotiated markets and, as discussed earlier in this chapter, they provide lower prices

or discounts for government, large firms, and other groups using hospital and physician services. Elizabeth Warren, who does research on the
relationship of health care costs and the uninsured, says that "there is
someone to negotiate on behalf of the insurance companies. There is
someone to negotiate on behalf of the state . . . but there is no one to
negotiate on behalf of people without insurance" (Lagnado 2003b, p. 1).
As in collective bargaining, there is a need for a bargaining agent. The
hospitals, for the most part, set their prices and discounts on the basis of
competing for buyers of services, especially in the era of managed care
companies. The government has its own set of specifications for pricing, which appear to make as much sense as subcommittees in academia.
More significantly, the uninsured have a higher rate of default on their
bills. Incidentally, this may identify the lack of a full connection between the uninsured and those without medical care. Many of the uninsured receive care. However, there have been aggressive attempts by the
hospitals and their collection agencies to force payment. There has not
been much success for these efforts. Some of these onerous bills for
low-income, uninsured patients are eventually negotiated on a one-to-
one basis without any brokers. Hospitals figure that something is better
than nothing. These private arrangements give little countenance to those
who suffer in this system. Some hospitals have policies for the uninsured. Some give discounts based on the ability to pay. Some have sub-
sidiary foundations that assure financial assistance for those who cannot
pay. Others have a sliding fee schedules directly related to household
income, and some provide, at least, partial payment from a state pool of
money collected from hospitals to offset "bad and uncollected debts" or
from state "charity pools" (Lagnado 2003b, p. 1).

One of the hidden causes of being uninsured is the mismatch of stag-
nant or decreasing middle-class incomes and the rising prices for health
insurance. Some of this mismatch is compounded by decreases in government subsidies for health insurance and the switch to lower-paying
jobs after the high-tech bust. In addition, some parents cannot afford to
pay the supplemental amount on their employer-based insurance to provide coverage for their children. Other families are caught in the middle-
income "squeeze" of having insufficient discretionary income to buy
health insurance and of having too high an income to qualify for a number of new state and federal subsidized programs. Counties and states
are struggling to meet the budgetary demands for Medicaid, the federal,
state, and local program of health insurance for the poor. This leaves the

counties and the states without budget funds to subsidize health care costs for middle-income households (Strom 2003, on-line pages).

Another suspect in the search for causes of the increase in the number of uninsured people in the United States is the effect of welfare reform on health insurance for low-income policies.

The major change in welfare policy came in 1996 with the enactment by Congress of the Personal Responsibility and Work Opportunity Reconciliation Act (PRWORA). The objective of the act was to decrease dependency of welfare assistance that provided categorical or entitlement status primarily to mothers with children living at home. The premise of the earlier Aid to Families with Dependent Children (AFDC) program was to provide financial support in the form of income assistance, food stamps, Medicaid, and other benefits. Employment was not required in order to receive the benefits. Indeed, welfare families before 1967 lost one dollar in benefits for every one dollar gained from working. Even though this ratio was changed in 1967 to losing two dollars in benefits for every three dollars gained from working (a number of allowances and disregards reduced the severity of the trade-off), the disincentives to leave welfare and go to work remained. Along with the issues of dependency and disincentives to work, there was a growing concern that women were not able to enjoy and benefit from being empowered in the work force. Given that one of the main exit routes from poverty was work, it became apparent that welfare ought to change. The PRWORA took as its goal to remove the AFDC population (mostly women and children) from the welfare assistance rolls and channel the adults toward jobs. The new law also provided the states with funds for assistance in job training and search as well as educational opportunities. The PRWORA continued assurances that the reform in welfare would not affect coverage of health insurance for those who left the welfare rolls (Kaestner and Kaushal 2003, pp. 959–981, on-line pages).

The studies of the effects of welfare reform on health insurance coverage are complicated by the fact that some people left the welfare rolls on their own initiative and others left under the influence of new laws. Further, some states gained permission from the federal government to experiment with welfare changes before the passage of the PRWORA. So the effects of welfare reform on health insurance is not clear. Those who left welfare voluntarily may have been induced to do so by the greater opportunities for work and education that were present in a growing economy. The study by Robert Kaestner and Neeraj Kaushal reviews the literature that generally supports the view of welfare reform as an agent of loss of health insurance for welfare leavers. However, Kaestner and Kaushal "take a more critical view of this evidence and argue that the widely held view that welfare reform resulted in a loss of health insurance is not well founded" (2003, on-line pages). Kaestner and Kaushal show that the "significantly smaller adverse consequences found here as compared to other studies weaken the argument that PRWOA and Medicaid [have] failed to provide insurance to low-educated women who have exited welfare" (2003, on-line pages). Some earlier studies have suggested that the loss of health insurance from welfare reform justifies an expansion of federal and state health insurance to assist those in need. This is a fundamental policy issue. It is disingenuous to argue that some failure to fully achieve a desired outcome, such as public health insurance coverage for welfare leavers, is due to insufficient public insurance. All we have to do is extend the publicly financed programs to solve the problem. This thinking ignores the presence of private insurance, particularly the employer-based programs available to most workers. This would include coverage for most single working mothers and low-educated workers. It would seem that the appropriate policy would be to assist welfare leavers in getting private insurance through their employers (Kaestner and Kaushal 2003, on-line pages).

Another rarely mentioned suspect in the search for clues to the increase in the number of the uninsured is the issue of required mandates. These mandates from federal and state government require an ever-expanding list of diseases or procedures to be covered by health insurance policies. These mandates have caused major increases in health insurance premiums. "According to a recent study by PricewaterhouseCoopers, mandates were responsible for 15 percent of the $67 billion increase in health spending in 2001. The Health Insurance Association of America estimates that mandates are the reason one in four uninsured Americans lacks coverage" ("Why You Can't Buy Insurance 2002, on-line pages). There is a very basic economic concept at work here: If more is to be covered by insurance, it will have to cost more. However, the cost is borne by those who cannot afford it or by those who would choose not to be covered by the larger list of mandated procedures. A clear policy implication is that if we have less insurance and more freedom to shop, we can choose among a menu of offerings. Medical savings accounts and the new health savings accounts might fill the bill nicely. (More about these in Chapters 6 and 7, on MSAs and Medicare, respectively.)

In New York State, every health insurance policy is required to have coverage for everything from alcoholism treatment, contraceptives, infertility services, off-label drug use, optometrists, podiatrists, and psychologists to social workers and much, much more! New York State has the highest health insurance costs in the nation. Are we surprised?

What Are the Consequences?

In both accounting and economic terms, what are the adverse effects of having over 43 million Americans without health care insurance? These effects will have an impact on the uninsured as well as on society itself. In addition to assessing the increase in out-of-pocket expenses of the uninsured, an economist is interested in the utilization of health services. Do the uninsured use fewer services or less of the relatively expensive resources? Are these the implicit costs of poor health and higher mortality rates? What is the value of foregone earnings and productivity? In general, we want to know both the explicit (accounting) costs and implicit (economic) costs. Economic costs are incurred when the value of an alternative use of resources is greater than the value of those resources in current use. It is the cost of doing one activity over another one. What are the trade-offs? Are there other consequences for all of us as a result of lack of insurance for some?

The principal finding of a study in 2000 found that "persons at midlife with job-related health benefits went on to spend only about $50 per year less in out-of-pocket payments for health services than persons who lacked health insurance. . . . However, they spent about $650 more per year in insurance premiums than the uninsured. The uninsured used relatively few health services . . . [but] when they were seriously ill . . . were likely to acquire public insurance" (Johnson and Crystal 2000, p. 911).

The costs of the uninsured are measured in terms of foregoing prevention care and routine physical exams. Facing catastrophic illnesses, many of the uninsured turn to various forms of public insurance. In other words, there is a redistribution effect of transferring the financing of these health care services to taxpayers, including the insured. The study by Richard Johnson and Stephen Crystal used data representing people at ages fifty-one to sixty-one or pre-retirement age (p. 211). Other consequences of the uninsured include increased mortality and morbidity rates, exposure to greater financial risk and uncertainty, and decreased value of health. The latter concept deals with health capital. Having more health capital means that there is more well-being and better function-ing of one's physical and mental capabilities. "Health capital is the present value of the utility resulting from a person's expected lifetime stock of health" (Miller, Vigdor, and Manning 2004, on-line pages). The healthier we are and the better we feel (well-being) about ourselves, the more productive we will be. This is part of a more general term, human capi-tal. This includes investments in education, job training, and health. The key term here is *investment*. The calculus of investment decisions is to have a net positive rate of return given the costs, including foregone earnings. Any rate of return on a particular investment such as subsidies for new clinics and medical personnel for low-income people would be expected to yield a higher rate of return than on alternative uses of the same funds. For policy purposes, we need to look at what economic costs have been incurred as a result of not making investments to re-duce, if not eliminate, the number of medically uninsured people. Ac-cording to a recent study, "the average uninsured person foregoes between $1,645 and $3,280 of health capital for each year without insurance cov-erage. . . . In the aggregate, for roughly forty million uninsured Ameri-cans, we estimate the value of health foregone per year without coverage at $65–$130 billion" (Miller, Vigdor, and Manning 2004, on-line pages).

Some estimates put the number of deaths of people aged twenty-five to sixty-four due to lack of insurance at 4,300 to 18,000 per year. On the basis of those estimates, "lack of health insurance [would be] the sixth-leading cause of death among people ages 25–64—after can-cer, heart disease, injuries, suicide and cerebrovascular disease but before HIV/AIDS or diabetes" (Davis 2003, p. 89S). These conse-quences of being uninsured can also be revealed in what would have been gained had there been an increase in insurance coverage. Karen Davis estimates that a reduction of 0.6 percent in the mortality rate could increase the gross domestic product of the United States by 66 billion dollars a year (Davis 2003, p. 89S). For the year 2001, 4.4 per-cent of insured Americans versus 15 percent of uninsured Americans had unmet needs for medical care. In 2001, cost was the major factor cited by 93.1 percent of the uninsured as the reason for unmet or de-layed medical care. This compares to 62 percent for the general popu-lation (Strunk and Cunningham 2002, on-line pages). Other costs of the uninsured include those borne by employees. Sick days result in 27 billion dollars of lost productive work (Davis 2003, p. 92S). Many of these costs are also transferred to taxpayers and the health system itself. In the health system, the "cost of providing uncompensated care to the uninsured totaled approximately $34.5 billion in 2001" (Davis 2003, p. 94S). The greater use of emergency rooms by the uninsured than by the insured increases the costs to hospitals. This is particularly true when alternative care at a clinic or physician's office would have been at a lower cost. However, the uninsured are more likely to use the emergency room than the insured even for routine or nonemergency care (Davis 2003, p. 94S). Taxpayers incur some of the costs of the uninsured through government payments for uncompensated care. The total bill for state, local, and federal payments, including Medicaid and Medicare, is approximately $23.6 billion a year. Other indirect costs are incurred by taxpayers when as a result of less work force participation and lower earnings by the uninsured, there is a decrease in tax payments. This decrease will ultimately be carried by taxpayers with significant effects on the payroll tax system for Social Security and Medicare. These programs are already preparing for the possibility that payroll tax revenues will be less than the benefits payouts as we reach the next decade or two (Davis 2003, pp. 95S, 96S).

Corrections and Choices for Policy

There are many issues that are interrelated with the social and personal consequences of having over 43 million Americans uninsured. That is, we face many gaps in our health care system, including the needs of the catastrophically ill, lack of physical or financial access, and lack of coverage for some services in our public and private insurance programs. Indeed, the increasing number of the uninsured places emphasis on the need for health care reform through subsidies and/or expansion of public and private insurance to cover the gaps. In turn, this raises questions about the equity, efficiency, and efficacy of public provision versus private provision of health care services. We explored some of these issues in the discussion of public and private goods in Chapter 2.

Do we want a universal health care system with the government as the single payer for health care services? This system would effectively end private insurance as we now know it. It would also suggest that competition in the market has no role, even for efficiency gains, in a health care system. Do we want a universal insurance system? One form of this would carry a mandate requiring everyone to purchase private insurance, with some assistance for low-income people. This system rests on the premise that competition among insurance companies would generate savings or efficiencies. This would mean that we would use fewer scarce resources that could be released to produce other public and private goods and services. While these proposals seem to encompass the extremes to which public policies can go to attract adherents, incremental reforms that provide some "middle zones" for compromise are likely to survive. We will examine all of these options in this section.

Incremental reforms differ depending on the political perspectives that guide the proposed policies. Jonathan Gruber provides an analysis of those reform options. Much of the analysis counters on shifting risk in health insurance. For those on the left side of the political spectrum, the preference is to expand public insurance to assume more responsibility for its role as a safety net. For those on the right side of the political spectrum, the preference is to subsidize the use of private insurance as a more efficient, consumer-choice mechanism (Gruber 2003, p. 271).

Given these political alignments, Gruber analyzes the likely impacts of three types of incremental expansion of health insurance. They are "tax credits for individual purchase of non-group insurance, expansions of public insurance to children and parents, and expansion of public insurance to all adults" (2003, p. 271). These types of insurance will be evaluated as to their ability to reduce the number of uninsured. However, there are possible consequences of expansion of public and private insurance coverage of the uninsured. Some of the privately insured population may change from existing insurance to a form of insurance that is receiving new and better subsidies. Others who are already privately insured may find a better deal with public insurance. In other situations, employees may find themselves with no employer-based insurance and no interest in other private insurance alternatives. That is, the employee may have dropped the insurance in light of newly subsidized programs. This is called the erosion of employee-based insurance. There also may be redistributional effects in favor of some groups such as the elderly, but at the expense of lower-age workers paying the Social Security and Medicare payroll tax (Gruber 2003, pp. 271–272).

These concerns about the effects of expansion of health insurance were codified by Gruber into five criteria (2003, pp. 273–276). These five criteria included those just cited plus the cost per newly insured person and the effects of expansion of insurance on the kinds or types of the uninsured that would gain from insurance expansion. For example, it might be profitable for firms to conceal their insurance coverage for employees when nongroup tax benefits are introduced. Also, it is likely that the healthy will take the option of a fixed credit amount for nongroup insurance coverage since their good health would then preclude any sizable expenditure on their part. Gruber finds that "the non-group expansions clearly cover a much healthier population on average" and that "expansion to adults with income up to 60 percent of the poverty line delivers virtually all the benefits to those below the poverty line" (2003, p. 275).

Gruber then compares the options of tax credit, expansion to adults, and expansion to parents based on his five criteria. He comes to an important policy choice; that is, "expanding insurance coverage through covering low-income adults is the dominant strategy. The only exception to this conclusion is for small expansions, where the cost per newly insured is highest for low-income adults . . . [but] an overwhelming advantage for expansions to adults per dollar of insurance costs covered . . . offsets this disadvantage" (2003, p. 276). We now have some sense of policy direction. We can see some relative preference for aid to very low-income people, particularly in expansion of insurance.

There are many others suggesting remedies for the uninsured ranging from universal care to universal insurance. At the far edges of the spectrum we range from the government making all rationing decisions and spending decisions in a single buyer of universal care system to a system of markets bringing competitive forces to reduce prices and give consumers more buying power. We have the latter system in a regulated form with negotiated markets under managed care. The government can exercise its regulatory role through anti-trust action or through administration of some prices in its Medicare and Medicaid program. The market system can provide a basis for consumer choice or shopping for a basket of health care services that brings the most satisfaction given the constraints of income and prices. This choice implies some consideration of more health care services than offered in a government package with even fewer health care services. One consumer may wish to switch preferences to non–health care services while another may shop carefully in order to add to a market basket with even more health care services. These possibilities become more viable than government-ordained coverage.

There are combinations of government and markets, as suggested by Gruber (2003). It is usually either markets or government that has the major role or, at least, the guiding hand. Many Americans are beginning to sense the need for some reform in the form of a major change. The change would be directed to provide more comprehensive care and less categorical assistance. Major reform would need to pay attention to the rising costs of medical care and insurance. It would have to have some strong effect on reducing the number of coinsured. Senator John Breaux, Democrat from Louisiana, chaired the National Bipartisan Commission on the Future of Medicare. He feels that we need a system "that combines the best care options offered by the private sector backed by the resources and oversight of Federal and State governments" (Breaux 2003, p. A14). This proposal is for a universal insurance system. In many ways, it maintains the market institutions of insurance firms and the private system of medical care providers, including physicians and hospitals. At the same time, the Breaux proposal has a major role for government as a catalyst for supplementing and subsidizing programs to fill in the gaps in our insurance programs. Senator Breaux calls for four guidelines for the new system: individual responsibility, guaranteed access to group health insurance, government responsibility ensuring Medicaid for vulnerable populations, and the provision of a valued role for employees. One of the key elements in the plan is the requirement that all Americans must buy, at least, a standard benefit medical insurance policy that would be specified by the government. This is a form of national health insurance. The government would provide subsidies or tax credits for low- and middle-income Americans. Children whose parents qualify for these subsidies would be eligible for a child wellness benefit package. Medicaid would continue its role providing assistance to those who are eligible. The proposal calls for a continuation of tax benefits for employee-based insurance (Breaux 2003, p. A14).

In the face of possible class-action lawsuits against some nonprofit hospitals, other hospitals are taking a preemptive path by voluntarily providing care to low-income people at almost no charge. The North Mississippi Health Systems in Tupelo, Mississippi, agreed to a ten-dollar visit for hospital services for four-person families with incomes less than $36,000 and 15 to 50 percent discounts from the Medicare charges for four-person families with incomes less than $72,000 (Johnston 2004, p. C2). These measures do not necessarily reflect a major change, but they are significant. First, most hospitals charge a higher rate for the uninsured than they do for the insured. Second, many of the uninsured are heavily in hospital debt and have little hope of getting services in the future. Under the North Mississippi Health System agreement, old debts cannot exceed 10 percent of family income. Given that hospitals collect very few debt payments from low-income people, the hospitals would not incur much of the expected $150 million of costs over the next ten years (Johnston 2004, pp. C2-C3).

Some other states have pools of funds from which to pay bad debts and charity cases. These pools are financed by charging hospitals a rate based on the size of their annual budget. Those hospitals with few bad debts or charity cases, in effect, subsidize those hospitals with large bad debts and many charity cases. Some not-for-profit hospitals have foundations that help finance some care for uninsured or low-income families. There are a number of laws and proposed laws in some states that force hospitals to reduce the high interest rates (10 percent in some cases) they charge on unpaid bills. In addition, there are reports of hospitals using very aggressive billing and collection techniques. Other proposed legislation would allow patients with incomes of up to four times the poverty rate to be offered rates lower than those for Medicare and Medicaid. The not-for-profit hospitals are caught between a rock and a hard place. They are tax exempt because of a pledge to be charitable, yet unpaid bills and lower revenue could put such hospitals into financial difficulty (Lagnado 2003c, pp. B1, B6).

The Institute of Medicine in a January 2004 report suggested guiding principles for any evaluation of proposals to solve or reduce the problems associated with the over 43 million Americans without health insurance. The principles are first, that health care coverage should be universal for all Americans. Second, health care should be continuous. Third, health care coverage should be affordable to all. Fourth, health care insurance should be affordable for society. This would require attention to the usual microeconomic concerns of cost-effective methods that produce the desired goals. This strategy would be successful, according to the Institute, if there is widespread financing from taxes, insurance premiums, and consumers. Fifth, the system should promote health and well-being through basic benefit packages and patient cost-sharing (Institute of Medicine 2004, pp. 1–5).

The National Coalition of Health Care also suggests a "move toward a health system in which every American has health insurance coverage" (Findlay and Miller 1999, on-line pages). Most of the research on health insurance reform over the years has emphasized the need to maintain an active role for private insurance. Mark Hall, in a 1994 study, noted the need to respect "both the social benefits of private insurance and its logic . . . in any attempt to rehabilitate the market for private health insurance" (Hall 1994, p. 94). The market mechanisms inherent in private insurance require risk taking. The assessment of risk creates incentives for risk reduction (Hall 1994, p. 94). This fundamental point is simply missing in the calls for single-buyer (government) universal care systems. Nevertheless, government subsidies, vouchers, and tax credits may be used to provide adequate access to the health care system. Economists and policymakers are still sorting out the effective ways to use market mechanisms and competitive incentives to produce affordable insurance but in a system where government has an oversight role for equity and efficacy.

However, there appears to be little support among policymakers and health economists for a single-payer, government universal health care system, particularly to solve the uninsurance problem. Every system has some rationing function. In the United Kingdom, kidney dialysis is rarely provided for people over the age of seventy-five under the National Health Care System. Even this system has introduced internal market-like mechanisms to produce some economies. Recently, the U.K. has allowed private funds to supplement national spending in order to meet the demand for health care (see Chapters 1 and 2). In Canada, one might have to wait months, if not years, in some provinces for elective surgery under the national health insurance system.

In the next chapter, we will undertake a study of a possible remedy for some of the uninsured. Medical savings accounts and, more recently, health savings accounts can make health insurance more affordable by combining high-deductible, low-premium insurance policies with savings accounts. The lower premiums provide greater access to health insurance. The savings accounts promote consumer choice and economizing on scarce resources. These accounts allow consumers to choose their own market basket of health care services rather than an arbitrary basic package of the one-size-fits-all system. We will also take up a number of uninsurance issues in Chapter 7 on Medicare reform.

6

Medical and Health Savings Accounts

Schemes That You Can Love!

The Setting: Filling the Gaps?

An interesting facet of American political, social, and economic life is that choices for policy decisions are open game for the many contenders for a central role in the eventual policy. Do we listen to the voices of the market? With roles for the market, whither the place of government? Do we recognize the need for the professionals in the field to assume some authority for the quality of services provided? Is a sovereign consumer able to deal with the asymmetry of information that favors the provider of care?

In this chapter, we have an unusual opportunity to say "yes" to all of these questions. Medical savings accounts (MSAs) and the new health savings accounts (HSAs) offer ways to test the proposition that consumers can be inspired to save for future medical expenses and to economize on current expenditures on health care. In theory, the consumer knows that a dollar saved today is a dollar plus the interest earned between the present and the future. For the consumer to save requires either a strong discipline (very rare among consumers in the United States) or some government assistance. If the consumer knows that the savings will not be taxed currently or in the future, there will be some incentive to save. Further, if the consumer is able to economize on health care spending and if the provider is conscious of the expenditure coming out-of-pocket, there could be considerable savings. These savings can be used to finance additional medical services. If there are tax-free contributions and tax-free withdrawals for medical care services, the government supports the concept that saving and shopping for one's own choice for a basket of medical services is a good idea.

This all means that the government and the market can have positive effects when working together for common goals. We also know that there are a number of gaps and needs in our own systems. We know that government subsidies and employer-based insurance have enabled many employees to purchase insurance. However, the subsidized insurance led to an increase in demand for insurance that, in turn, caused an increase in demand for health care with a consequent increase in health care expenditures.

In recent years, many employees have increased the cost-sharing responsibilities for their employees. This has caused more out-of-pocket expenditures, putting new pressures on already constrained family budgets. Employees are often forced to look for part-time or moonlighting work in places that do not have adequate insurance coverage.

We do have gaps in our health care system. They include the uninsured, the underinsured, the overinsured, and lack of sufficient access to health care for the poor and, sometimes, middle-income people. This access problem is both financial and physical. As discussed in Chapter 5, on the uninsured, the insufficient financial resources can lead to health care needs being neglected or delayed. These problems are compounded by serious inadequacies in the distribution of medical resources. This brief exploration of the nation's health care woes is intended to provide the context for the role of medical or health savings accounts. From a policy perspective, the creation of the new HSAs under the Medicare Prescription Drug, Improvement and Modernization Act of 2003 (Public Law No. 108–173) represents a major government initiative to promote savings, consumer empowerment, and economies in the financing and delivery of health care. A clear inference is that the government is depending upon market forces to solicit consumer preferences for individual baskets of health care services. These choices are guided by consumers rather than by government, which would generally favor a "one-size-fits-all" basket of health services. Rather than government being the arbitrator of which health care services to finance, government becomes the *enabler* for consumers to determine what to buy, how much to save, and how to buy only the insurance that is needed.

Instead, all of these incentive health care plans have similar intent and effect. We will explore the "devils in the details" of these various plans in the next section. The purpose of this discourse is to counterface health care reform of a "market-like" type aided by incentives through the tax codes with a universal health care system that features a single payer/buyer (a government agency) with no incentives to save. This will provide us with the general framework and perspective for a further analysis of our health care system.

Beyond the details are the connections, sometimes referred to as the "connecting of the dots." In any kind of a systematic change of our ailing health care system, we need to explore the impact of one change in one part of the system on any other part or feature of the system. If we lessen the impact of decision making by managed care organizations (MCOs), we may expect that there is less of a constraint on rising health care prices and expenditures. If we reduce subsidies for insurance, we may find that some of the most needy people have less insurance and less access to the system. Medical savings accounts and health savings accounts will place more emphasis on marketplace choices and savings as investments for the future; however, people with low incomes may have difficulty in funding the savings accounts even with reduced premiums on high-deductible insurance policies. The safety net of social programs will play a significant role in any policy decisions.

What, if any, effect will HSAs and MSAs have on research and technology? The more general question is, do market-driven forms of competition aid or abet technology advancement? In theory, pure competition in product markets induces firms to use state-of-the-art technology or face the consequences of an exit from the market. However, without profits in the long run, firms are unable or unwilling to invest in new or advanced technology. This is at the heart of a struggle to make our system more competitive, particularly for international trade, so that we can enjoy more diverse products at affordable prices. As with pharmaceutical prices in the United States, more competitive prices might result in reduced amounts of new pharmaceuticals and other medical research, innovation, and development.

As consumers bring competitive pressure on prices of medical services and products, will there be trade-offs of lower quality? Much of this has been somewhat answered with respect to the influence of MCOs on costs, quality, and technology. However, the differences between MCOs and MSAs/HSAs are significant. Individuals are often outside the contracts negotiated between HMOs and providers. In a sense, the employer negotiates on behalf of the employees, but it is the employer that makes the decisions. In MCOs, there are barriers between the employee and the price paid for health services. The employee has virtually no say on a health insurance or health care package except for the choices offered by the MCO as agreed to by the employer or human resource department. The employee may add options or spouse inclusion, but only from a limited menu. Another separation, aided by HMOs, is that the price paid to the supplier is different than the price the employee pays for services. The other significant barrier between the employee and the price paid for health care services is the lack of individual choice. This choice is evident in MSAs and HSAs. Within the deductible amount and the amount funded by employee, employer, and/or government into the savings accounts, the employee can pick an individual package of health services that maximizes utility (satisfaction) given the constraints of prices and consumer budgets. Under these circumstances, the price paid by the employee for a health care service is more likely to correspond with the price charged by the provider. That is, the marginal utility (satisfaction) for the last unit of a service (e.g., a visit to a physician) purchased by a consumer subject to constraints of budgets is likely to correspond to the marginal value of the physician's service. In a fee for service for the physician and an out-of-pocket expense or withdrawal from a savings account for the customer, we come near to closing the gap between buyer and seller. If this exchange between physician and consumer is consummated on the previously described basis, a gain in welfare is obtained. At least one of the two parties to the arrangement is better off after the exchange, and the other party is no worse off. This represents a gain in efficiency.

Absent the preceding barriers, these types of exchanges are only possible in a market context. The tax code, particularly for the new health savings accounts, provides special tax treatment. This treatment from the government allows and encourages these exchanges. The exchanges themselves work through markets. The consumer gets a more tailored package. The physician accepts a fee that reflects the value, at the margin, of the health services rendered. This fee may be less than a fee negotiated with an MCO, given the reduced paperwork. There are potential savings for employers in MSA/HSA plans. These savings can then be used for other employee benefits and for postponed capital investments.

MSAs and HSAs: What Are They?

In addition to the medical savings accounts and health savings accounts, there are a number of "half-breed," or similar, plans. All of these can be called "incentive plans" in the sense of market forces as described earlier.

These plans include the health reimbursement arrangement (HRA), Whole Foods' consumer-driven plan, health savings security accounts (HSSA), wellness programs, and flexible spending accounts (FSAs).

A medical savings account provides government assistance to consumers through a tax-free savings account to be used to pay for routine medical care. The MSA is combined with a high-deductible health insurance policy that has a lower premium than policies without deductibles or with lower deductibles. Individuals with MSAs rely on the savings accounts to pay for medical expenses up to the deductible amount. If the savings accounts have insufficient funds to pay for the deductible amounts, then consumers would have to pay out of pocket for the differences. Some variations of these MSAs use tax credits, vouchers, and subsidies from the government to finance deductible amounts for low-income people. Other MSAs allow employers to fund the employees' accounts. Some of these employees' contributions are derived from savings in premium costs with high-deductible policies.

Health savings accounts were created under the Medicare Prescription Drug Improvement and Modernization Act of 2003. This law included a section to the Internal Revenue Code that provided tax-favored benefits for purchasers of HSAs for tax years beginning after December 31, 2003 (DeScherer and Myers 2004, pp. 3–14). These accounts were "designed to help individuals save for future qualified medical and retiree health expenses on a tax-free basis" (U.S. Department of the Treasury [hereafter U.S. Treasury] 2004a, on-line pages). These HSAs can also be used to pay for current medical expenses. The general expectation is that the new HSAs will replace the MSAs. The original MSAs, known as Archer Medical Savings Accounts, began as a pilot program in 1996 and had very restrictive requirements for enrollment. They were limited to the self-employed and employees of small businesses. The law that created these accounts allowed for only 750,000 policies by the end of 2003. Holders of MSAs can keep them or roll them over to HSAs. However, as of December 2003, only 70,000 policies had been issued. In contrast, under the newly created HSAs, individuals and/or employers can contribute to these accounts ("A Comeback for MSAs" 2003, on-line pages; and Goodman 2003, on-line pages).

There are considerable tax benefits for these sheltered accounts. These HSAs allow tax-free contributions and withdrawals. The employer and employee are allowed to collectively contribute up to the amount of the health plan deductible but no more than $2,600 for individuals and $5,150 for families. These figures will be indexed for inflation on an annual basis (Lueck 2003, pp. D1, D4).

A major feature of HSAs is that the contributed amounts belong to the individuals who acquire them. The HSAs are portable, making them a formidable defense against declining availability of full employer-based coverage and the vicissitudes of labor markets. In a similar fashion to IRAs, any of the funds that are not spent can remain in the account for use in future years and accrue interest and be tax-free. Contributions can be made by an individual or family member. These are tax-deductible whether or not the individual itemizes deductions on the federal income tax return. The employer can make contributions to the HSA of any employee. Neither the employee nor the employer is taxed on the employer's contribution. Employers that have cafeteria plans can allow employees to contribute part of their salary, which is reduced for tax purposes. For example, if an employee contributes $2,000 of a $40,000 salary to a HSA, the reduced salary of $38,000 is then subject to federal tax. Any withdrawals from the HSA are not subject to tax if used to pay for medical expenses that qualify under the law. If the withdrawals are for expenses that do not qualify, they will be taxed and subject to a penalty. This is for people under the age of sixty-five and not disabled. Qualified expenses include dental and vision care but not cosmetic procedures. People over the age of fifty-five up to the time of eligibility for Medicare can make additional contributions to the HSA allowances identified earlier. These additional contributions vary according to the year of the contribution. For the year 2004, the amount is $500. The amount increases each year by $100 until the year 2009. After 2009, the additional contribution is limited to $1,000 (U.S. Treasury 2004a, on-line pages).

In order to qualify for HSAs, individuals must purchase a high-deductible health plan (HDHP) and *not* be covered by another insurance policy. This requirement provides the basis or complementary part for the HSA to be fully operative as a low-cost medical savings plan. The HDHP is defined as a health insurance plan with a minimum deductible of $1,000 for individuals and $2,000 for a family. This high-deductible plan assures a lower premium than would be available under a comprehensive plan, particularly one with no deductibles or low co-payments.

Once individuals reach the age of sixty-five, any amounts in an HSA can be used for health expenses to pay premiums for Part B of Medicare, Medicare HMOs, or the employee's part of certain other health insurance premiums. The remaining HSA funds may *not* be used to buy a Medigap policy. Any of these excess HSA funds that are used for medical expenses may be withdrawn without being taxed. There will be a tax on any withdrawals used for other expenses (U.S. Treasury 2004a, on-line pages).

The HSA and HDHP programs are designed to help both employees and employers obtain low-cost health insurance for major health care costs and to provide a basis for saving for future routine medical expenses. Once established, the HSAs lend themselves to a more consumer-directed, less bureaucratic system in which the government assists the empowered citizen. The National Federation of Independent Business (NFIB) claims that "savvy NFIB members can lower costs for themselves, their employees and their families with newly enacted Health Savings Accounts (HSAs)" ("Cut Out the Costly Co-Pays" 2004, p. 46). Small business owners find themselves reducing other benefits, capital investments, or business needs in order to finance health care costs or insurance. According to Paul Fronstin, director of health research and education of the Employee Benefit Research Institution, "It's not just about what health care costs, it's about the other trade-offs that come along with that cost" (Bannan 2004, p. 32). The HSAs offer a solution with the HDHPs that offer lower premiums than standard comprehensive plans. The lower premiums reflect lower risk. An employer can lower the HDHP premium even more by increasing the deductible. There are tax savings through HSAs for both employers and employees (Bannan 2004, pp. 32, 34).

The following example illustrates potential tax benefits. A $2,000 contribution to an HSA would produce estimated savings that vary with adjusted gross income (AGI). The tax benefit for an AGI of $35,000 would be $200; for a $50,000 AGI, it would be $300; for a $150,000 AGI, $615; for a $500,000 AGI, a savings of $721. These figures are based on a married couple with two children in the year 2004 (Lueck 2003, pp. D1, D4). Any investment and interest income that occurs to the holder of an HSA are tax-free. Upon the death of the holder, the HSA can be transferred to the spouse without being taxable. Alternately, the HSA can be a taxable inheritance. Some critics feel that the young, healthy, and wealthy will adversely affect the risk pool for comprehensive insurance and for health maintenance organizations (HMOs). Older and higher-risk individuals tend to dominate the risk pool (Lueck 2003, p. D4).

The combination of tax-advantaged savings plans and high-deductible insurance polices has prompted national financial firms to work closely or merge forces with insurance firms to market the HSAs. In the meantime, those firms with experience in selling the Archer Medical Savings Accounts have a head start. *Inside Consumer-Directed Care,* a trade news letter published by Atlantic Information Services, Inc., reports that "business is booming . . . [for] financial groups that have been selling the accounts" (*Inside Consumer-Directed Care* 2004, p. 2). Some feel that the HSA will give legitimacy, recognition, and acceptance to the notion of saving for medical needs that is consumer directed. This is really the original idea that inspired medical savings accounts (MSAs).

The health reimbursement arrangement (HRA) is another example of a consumer-driven health plan. In concept, HRAs follow the pattern of medical and health savings plans in providing health care savings accounts. But the amounts that can be contributed, the control of the account, the portability, and the tax advantages vary significantly between HRAs and HSAs. In June 2002, the Internal Revenue Service announced new regulations that gave HRAs the necessary impetus for acceptability. HRAs, as with other consumer-driven plans, require high deductibles. These deductibles are somewhat offset by employers' contributions to employees' individual cash accounts. Employers, in particular, are pleased at the opportunity to have a decrease in health insurance premiums for their employees. However, the employer has more control of the HRAs than is the case with HSAs. Specifically, while employers and employees are allowed to make tax-advantaged contributions to an HSA, only employers can establish accounts under an HRA. The HSAs are for current and future medical expenses. The HRAs are designed to allow employees to be reimbursed for eligible medical expenses paid out of pocket. The funds not expended in any one year can be rolled over to following years of an HRA. Under HSAs, any funds not spent may remain in the savings account and earn interest. The HSAs are portable from job to job; the HRAs are not portable. Under HRAs, reimbursements made by employers are not subjected to federal taxation. As indicated in our analysis of HSAs, any contributions to the savings plans by the employer or the employee are tax deductible ("Business Owners Find Options" 2004, p. 2). Any reimbursement paid to a worker under HRAs is not treated as income (Fogarty 2003, p. 6A). The incentives in HRAs are such that consumers might treat the funds in their savings accounts as their own and hence be more economical in their spending on health care. Under managed care organizations, the "system of small co-payments . . . isolates consumers from the true costs of health care. To encourage employees to avoid unnecessarily expensive treatments and visits to emergency rooms, marketers of these plans [HRAs] offer features like web sites, nurse help lines and detailed information on generic drugs" (Kobliner 2003, p. 8BU). As with other consumer-directed plans, there is concern that the risk pool for more comprehensive policies will be adversely affected by the healthier, wealthier, and younger people moving to HSAs and HRAs.

The Whole Foods Market, Inc., "consumer-driven" health care plan is another variation of the theme of consumer incentives for economizing on health care expenses, particularly for routine expenses. This plan has *no* premiums for individual workers who have been with Whole Foods for a few months. There are premiums for spouses and children, which disappear after five years of full employment. However, there are high deductibles of $500 for prescriptions and $1,000 for other medical expenses. To offset those deductibles, the company deposits from $300 to $1,800 in employee accounts. The deposits vary depending on how long employees have worked for Whole Foods. After the deductible is met, the plan pays for about 80 percent of most other medical expenses. The employees can roll over any remaining funds in the savings accounts for future years. Indeed, the workers at Whole Foods had $14 million left in their savings accounts by the end of 2003. Further, health care claims decreased by 13 percent and hospital admissions decreased by 22 percent from the previous year. The participation in this plan by the workers was up to 95 percent of eligible workers by 2004. The workers did trade off reductions and eliminations in benefits in order to obtain this new program. The employees at Whole Foods are on average younger and healthier than those in other companies. This may account for some of the differences in the success of this plan as compared to others, and reflects some of the concerns about consumer-oriented health plans (Lieber 2004, p. A1).

Wellness programs, especially those that incorporate rewards in the form of reductions in health insurance premiums, offer another approach to consumer-directed or incentive plans. One example of these plans is that of Creation Technologies of Oak Creek, Wisconsin. The employees share savings with their employer on health insurance premiums through a wellness program called the Hundred Percent Club. They "earn points for each healthy action they take, such as getting an annual physical exam. . . . Those who achieve 100 points get a premium reduction from the insurer, as does the employer" ("Healthy Habits" 2004, p. 35). Some of these more successful programs provide the cultural and physical environment conducive to good health. These include fitness centers and team and focus groups that solicit ideas from workers. Some wellness programs offer a separate side fund for self-insurance to encourage fewer claims. The Office of Education in Mendocino County, California, adopted a $500-deductible plan from Blue Shield in place of a no-deductible plan in the late 1970s. The premium savings to the employer allowed the development of a side fund to self-insure the first $500 of claims for each employee. Any part of the $500 side fund that was *not* used by the employee for claims would accrue to the worker upon leaving work or retirement. The purpose was to allow unused portions of insurance to be available for future cash payments and to encourage healthier habits for workers and, consequently, to have more productive workers (Heffley and Miceli 1998, pp. 445–446).

A flexible spending account (FSA) is another form of consumer-directed care or incentive plan that combines market mechanisms with government-provided tax benefits. These accounts are available to workers at the initiative or discretion of employers. In the typical plan, the employee exercises an option to establish an FSA by contributing pre-tax dollars through a reduction in salary. The FSAs are accounts funded by workers, whose contributions are tax-exempt. Often, the FSAs are part of cafeteria plans in which workers take a fixed sum of dollars from their employers. Individually, the workers choose how to allocate these monies among choices of day care, elder care, spouse benefits, life insurance, health insurance, and other benefits. In some plans, workers may choose a health plan that is less comprehensive and hence less expensive. This choice would release some funds for other benefits (Martin 1998, p. 227). This allows individuals to tailor their spending accounts based, in part, on their health status. Those who are in better-than-average health may choose to spend less on conventional health care and more on non–health care items, such as day care. Further, those who have allocated a considerable portion of their flexible spending amount to health benefits may spend more of the benefits on maintenance or preventative care rather than on needs or wants for current incidences of minor illness. Employees would have the incentive to choose cost-effective plans in terms of their own ranking of preferences constrained by the amount of the benefit (budget) and the relative prices of the various choices (Martin 1998, p. 227). There are several variations of these flexible spending plans, but typically the worker will forfeit any remaining funds in the account at the end of the year. Further, there is no interest paid on any of the remaining funds (Fogarty 2003, p. 6A).

All of these incentive-based, consumer-directed health plans have significant concepts in common. Most importantly, they tend to "replace more comprehensive coverage with catastrophic or high-deductible coverage, coupled with stronger personal incentives to prudently utilize routine care and to adopt a healthier lifestyle" (Heffley and Miceli 1998, p. 445). Some major employers are considering the "stacking" of these plans. This strategy might attract firms that operate with large groups. If this happens, HSAs could become the vehicle for viable employer-based health care. In turn, this would vitalize the private insurance market and empower consumers (*Inside Consumer-Directed Care* 2004, pp. 1 and 7). Perhaps this emphasis on market forces to reduce costs and to tailor consumer benefits on an individual basis will erode political forces that favor a national insurance or national coverage program. According to Regina Herzlinger of Harvard Business School, a consumer-directed individual health insurance program will eventually replace the current program, which is based on employer coverage of health benefits (*Inside Consumer-Directed Care* 2004, pp. 4–6). This movement for consumer direction might move the consumer and the provider closer together, especially in terms of the price for a given service. Currently, the price that the consumer pays is set separately from the price that the provider is willing to accept. The consumer is insulated from influencing the price he or she ultimately pays by insurance, subsidies, managed care contracts, monopolies, government-directed programs, and benefit packages of employers. Further, the consumer is effectively prevented from choosing the quantity of services and/or the length of the services provided. We may well evolve into something close to individual insurance that will be independent of employment. We should expect a wide range of insurance plans from employers in order to stay competitive in the labor markets. Quality control, disease management, and genetic research allow a close match of one's health condition and risk or insurance needs (*Inside Consumer-Directed Care* 2004, pp. 4–6). We should expect some serious inroads to conventional group insurance policies from these consumer-directed plans.

Medical Savings Accounts, The Generic Model: The Genesis of the New Political Economy of Health Care

What is the basic generic nature of medical savings accounts? What has formed the genesis of their arrival into the political economy of health care? Even though it appears that the new health savings accounts will subsume the MSAs, it is the latter that represents the model. That is, the notion of individual choices in both health care and insurance programs inherent in medical savings accounts frames this discussion on public or government versus private or market initiatives for health care policy. Whether the question is the price, the premium, or who pays, MSAs offer a new path to policy decisions.

The genius for MSAs came from John C. Goodman and Gerald L. Musgrave in a pathbreaking book titled *Patient Power,* first published in 1992. The authors make the point that "health care costs are rising because, for individual patients, medical care is cheap, not expensive . . . patients pay only 5 cents out-of-pocket for every dollar they spend in hospitals . . . [and] less than 19 cents out-of-pocket for every dollar they spend on physicians' services, and they pay less than 24 cents out of every dollar they spend on health care of all types" (Goodman and Musgrave 1992, p. vii). In other words, the consumer is not fully constrained by the price of health care. Therefore, the consumer is likely to spend more on health care than if the full price were charged. It seems as if whatever is subsidized, we get more of it. This is a point that escapes most of the public debate on health care. People have an array of choices, not only for health care services but also for other goods and services. Each of us has a different selection for an individual basket of goods and services. Within these baskets, we consciously or unconsciously rank our selections in priority order. But our ordinal scales of preferences are subjected to the reality of the prices in the marketplace and the limitations of our incomes. What is "in the pocket" permits us to make choices among goods and services. However, if the government effectively lowers the prices of medical services, we spend more on those services.

Currently, we tend to save little, if any, of our current incomes for future medical expenses. Certainly one factor is the small out-of-pocket expenses that we incur as consumers for current health care services. However, "we" do spend a lot on health care as taxpayers, business firms, and consumers. Aided and abetted by government subsidies, we buy insurance and health care in amounts greater than we would have in the absence of government assistance. The public (government) share for funding health care expenditures is almost one-half of the total. If we add the effects of government subsidies, tax credits, and directed care, the government share is well over one-half of all health care expenditures. With all of this, plus the role of insurance and managed care organizations in determining the prices, types of care, and amounts of medical care, there is a clear separation between what the consumer pays for health care and what the consumer receives in value. At the end of the day, the consumer pays more and receives something less in value and quantity than would have been available in a normal market setting. Prices have been administered, quantities have been limited, and choices rationed through government, institutional, and insurance mechanisms. The consumer is not sovereign and, certainly, is not empowered. As a nation, we have been experiencing rising health care expenditures. Part of this phenomenon is attributable to the basic desire of Americans to demand more health care as their incomes rise. Economists call this a *normal* good. This is a good whose consumption rises as incomes of consumers increase.

The rationing of health care in the United States comes as a direct result of consumers being constrained by their incomes and the prices of health care services. That is, consumers cannot fully satisfy their preferences for health care services, even with rising incomes. This applies mostly to out-of-pocket expenses and fits well with free and competitive market exchanges. Also, we know that those consumers who are either unable or unwilling to pay for health care services are excluded from the benefits of these services. It is the exclusion rule for private goods and services. We know that the demand for health care services is relatively price inelastic (having a numerical coefficient of less than one (< 1); as the price increases, the quantity demanded decreases less than proportionately). In the survey of selected studies presented in *Health Economics and Policy,* a textbook by James W. Henderson, the price elasticities for hospital admissions were in the range of -0.32 to -0.46, hospital length of stay in the range of -0.06 to 0.29, medical care in the range of -0.22 to -0.75, and physician office visits in the range of -0.08 to -0.10 (Henderson 2002, p. 160). In all of these cases, the percentage change in quantity demanded was less than proportional (< 1) to the change in the price of the medical service. Two factors may explain most of this phenomenon. One is the unique characteristic of health care referred to in the introductory chapter, that of the asymmetry of information about health care that favors the provider over the consumer. A second unique feature of health care is the use of third parties (other than buyer or seller) in the financing of health care. This is significant when we analyze the potential effects of medical or health savings plans. Most of the effects can be measured in terms of the effects of co-payments from the insured on their demand for health care services.

The Rand Health Insurance Study, as reported in Henderson (2002), demonstrated that consumers have different price elasticities of demand depending on the degree of cost sharing in different insurance plans. Using estimates derived from studies, price elasticity was −0.17 for no cost sharing, −0.22 for coinsurance of 25 percent to 95 percent for overall medical care, "ranging from −0.14 for hospital care to −0.43 for preventive care. The amount demanded for those provided with free medical care was about 50 percent higher than for those who had to pay 95 percent of the total cost" (Henderson 2002, pp. 162–163). To some, this may be intuitively obvious. We might be expected to purchase more health care or more health insurance as the share that consumers pay declines. The point of this discourse is to illustrate that consumers may be buying more health insurance and health care services than they really need or want. Consequently, both the premiums for health insurance and the prices for health care service rise. In turn, health insurance and health care services become less accessible, particularly for low-income people. For employers, the rising price of health insurance crowds out other employee benefits and employers ask for more co-payments from employees. The problem becomes compounded by job losses or changes in jobs that often cause loss of insurance, reduced benefits, or larger co-payments for workers. In spite of the best (and sometimes, the worst) efforts of employers, employees, MCOs, and government to make health care more affordable and more accessible, the opposite often happens.

Milton Friedman, Nobel Prize (economics) laureate, believes that the role of third parties, including government, employees, and insurance companies, has caused both dissastisfaction by patients and high costs of medical care. Patients are separated from the decisions on what to buy and how much to spend on medical care. In Friedman's words, "nobody spends someone else's money as wisely or as frugally as he spends his own" (Friedman 2001, p. 43). There is a similar effect with tax exemption on medical costs through employer-based health insurance. The managed care company, employer, or insurance company arranges the type and quantity of health care for the employees. This suggests that the employees are not in control of their own medical care spending. Also, this "leads employees to take a larger fraction of their total remuneration in the form of medical care than they would if spending on medical care had the same tax status as other expenditures" (p. 45).

Friedman is also concerned about the peculiar nature of health care insurance as compared to other forms of insurance. With other forms of casualty and liability insurance, we tend to protect against major losses whose probability of occurrence is low. These catastrophic losses are beyond financial reach when they occur; hence, we tend to insure against them. However, we tend to "rely on insurance to pay for regular medical examinations and often for prescriptions" (Friedman 2001, p. 47). The effect of this reliance on insurance and the effect of state and federal governments on coverage of routine medical care under Medicare and Medicaid has been to increase the cost of health insurance. This has also led to less consumer choice of medical care services. Ironically, these same forces have caused many to be uninsured. By Friedman's reckoning, "the tax-exemption on medical spending accounts for 57 percent of the increased cost of medical care over the last 80 years, while the Medicare and Medicaid system accounts for 43 percent" (p. 43). Friedman suggests that, in the absence of these tax exemptions, Medicare, and Medicaid, health insurance markets would have targeted catastrophic insurance as a large insurable risk (p. 48). This logic, which arose before its political time, is now an integral part of the newly legislated health savings accounts. Some of the earlier proposals for national health insurance also focused on the need for catastrophic insurance, often combined with coverage for the poor. This approach was best illustrated in the Long-Ribicoff Bill introduced in the United States Senate in 1973. This bill had three provisions:

(1) a catastrophic expense provision that would assist all persons covered by social security;
(2) a plan to replace Medicaid by paying virtually all basic medical expenses of low-income people regardless of welfare eligibility, employment status, or family composition; and
(3) provisions to promote the sale of standard health insurance policies to the non-poor. (Davis 1975, pp. 85–86).

There were a series of co-payments and deductibles for the catastrophic part of the bill—which was to have been financed by the regressive payroll tax. The third part of the bill was included to help finance the deductibles for catastrophic coverage. This would come in the form of private insurance policies certified by the U.S. Department of Health, Education, and Welfare (Davis 1975, pp. 85–89). This earlier proposal, which never became law, is similar to the reform for the Health Savings Accounts (HSAs) passed by the Congress in 2003. The HSAs have to be combined with catastrophic insurance with high deductibles or a high-deductible health plan.

The Long-Ribicoff plan for catastrophic coverage was restricted to those who have Social Security benefits, mostly people over the age of sixty-five. Friedman's proposal for catastrophic coverage is different than the old national insurance plans. It is more comprehensive. Friedman's more radical program would end enrollments to Medicare and Medicaid. It would provide for catastrophic insurance coverage combined with a high-deductible plan for all families. It would also end all tax advantages for employer-based health plans. Except for the tax incentive, this is similar to the recently legislated HSAs combined with HDHPs. The major difference is that the new program in the United States is designed for people *under* the age of sixty-five. Under Friedman's less radical program, medical savings accounts could be used to finance Medicare and Medicaid. This proposal would induce the participants to use their savings accounts for routine medical services without reliance on third parties. The insurance part would be directed toward the financing of major medical expenses. Further, Friedman believes that medical savings accounts would restore faith in markets and the efficiency of our private enterprise system "to improve the quality and lower the cost of medical care" (Friedman 2001, pp. 54–55).

The Economic Effects of Consumer- and Incentive-directed Health Care

Incentive-based health plans and their close cousins, consumer-directed health plans, are inclusive of the variety of plans that are identified in the previous section. These plans include medical savings accounts and the new health savings accounts. In this section, the emphasis is on the goals of these plans as they are interfaced with likely outcomes. The possible outcomes or effects of these plans have been identified and subjected to a number of economic analyses. Some of the studies reviewed in this chapter offer comparisons with effects of the more traditional methods of health insurance. Questions and issues raised include the effects of incentive-based plans on consumer behavior, particularly with respect to the desire for preventative care. Also, what are the benefits for consumers of these plans? Will the health savings accounts benefit the wealthy and the healthy at the expense of the low-income and ill population (Heffley and Miceli 1998, pp. 445–447)?

A study by Dennis R. Heffley and Thomas J. Miceli first sets the context for exploring these issues. The major finding in looking at the constrasting comprehensive plans (nonincentive) is that "full coverage of treatment causes under-investment in health activities" (1998, p. 462). They found that, under the basic incentive-based insurance plan, individuals will "select socially efficient levels of health activities" (p. 462). This finding will work best when the insurer uses an experience rating rather than a community rating system. In this plan, the insurer can vary the premium based on the differences in health status among the insured. The system depends on the establishment of an expected target level of expenditures by consumers. There are rewards and refunds for the insured individuals who now have an incentive for maintaining their health care expenditures below the targeted amount. This is an example of how the economics of insurance, adverse risk selection, consumer choice, healthy lifestyles, disease management, and costs of illness combine in an effective incentive plan that promotes wellness subject to varying degrees of psychological or consumer behavior. The Heffley and Miceli study also finds that incentive plans do not necessarily adversely affect the less healthy individuals. In addition to the investment in health activities, the incentive plan tends to promote the use of preventative care to a socially optimal level (p. 463).

Another study posits a more negative outcome for medical savings accounts that are combined with high-deductible health insurance plans. A 1999 study by Daniel Zabinski, Thomas M. Selden, John F. Moeller, and Jessica S. Banthin, published in the *Journal of Health Economics,* suggests that MSAs "will tend to crowd out comprehensive coverage" (Zabinski et al. 1999, p. 215). This is an oft-mentioned criticism of incentive-based plans. The thinking is that the highly tax-advantaged medical and health savings accounts will have a major effect on enrollment over the comprehensive plans. The consequence of significant shifts from comprehensive plans to incentive-based plans could cause premiums to increase for the former. This effect is based on the expected decrease in the number of healthy individuals in the comprehensive insurance risk pools. If all families with employment-based insurance plans were to switch from comprehensive coverage to MSAs (with high-deductible policies), the "aggregate effect of reform may be positive, although gains from reductions in medical expenditures and third-party administrative expenses are at least partially offset by increased exposure to risk and by deadweight losses associated with tax revenue losses" (p. 215). Appropriately, the authors note that there is great variation among families with respect to those who would gain and those who would lose by adopting medical savings plans as their insurance/health care vehicles. Zabinski and his co-authors are especially concerned about their findings that poor and families with newly born children would probably lose the most if medical savings plans were adopted for the nation. Further, "high risk families are worse off compared to their pre-reform well being, facing higher expected out-of-pocket medical expenses along with greater exposure to risk" (p. 215).

Another study, by Larry Ozanne, suggests that if the nonelderly represented in his cross-section analysis were to enroll in a medical savings account with a high-deductible health plan by dropping the more comprehensive plan, "they would reduce their medical spending by between 2 percent and 8 percent" (Ozanne 1996, p. 225). These reductions would stem from the initial expectation that catastrophic insurance alone would change consumer behavior. The more routine medical expenses would have to be paid for out of pocket and that would reduce expenditures on these items. If the MSA is combined with an HDHP, the reduction in spending by the insured could be significantly higher. Ozanne reports on some employers using these MSAs without *any* tax preferences. Apparently, the employers experienced larger reductions in the expenses of their firms relative to the reductions in the medical spending of their employees than was evident in the Ozanne study. Ozanne reports that another study indicated that aggregate health spending in the United States would decrease by almost 28 percent if there were a 100 percent enrollment of the population that had current private health insurance (Ozanne 1996, p. 235).

Dana P. Goldman, John L. Buchanan, and Emmett B. Keeler analyzed the effects of small businesses using MSAs on the type of insurance and the amount of insurance coverage (Goldman, Buchanan, and Keeler 2000, pp. 53–74). The simulation model used predicted spending by families in fee-for-service (FFS), HMOs, MSAs, and no insurance plans. These plans were then assigned premiums with firm-specific costs included. These simulated models suggested that the MSAs offered by small business would be attractive to 56 percent of all employees. The study also found that MSAs would be attractive to employees of small business firms that provided health maintenance or traditional fee-for-service plans. However, the MSAs would not be overly attractive to firms that currently provide insurance for their employees. This finding is consistent with empirical results from other studies that are referenced in the Goldman, Buchanan, and Keeler study. This study also found, contrary to other studies, that MSAs did not attract the healthy, low-risk individuals who elected to be uninsured. The welfare gains would show slight improvement. Tax revenue effects to government with losses in MSA deposits would be balanced by smaller premium payments of firms (2000, pp. 53, 71).

Medical savings accounts may reduce the demand for conventional health care such as physician visits. Many people may prefer visits to chiropractors, nutritionists, exercise professionals, or diet clinics over the traditional forms of medicine. The conventional or traditional forms of care are more commonly insured and, hence, require fewer out-of-pocket expenses. Further, if one has insurance, there is not any real financial advantage in paying for conventional care to the extent it is a substitute for alternative care. Also, medical savings accounts are expected to promote savings and to reduce health expenditures. Early employer experiences with MSAs provide only a limited perspective since these early incentive plans were very restrictive. This small sample demonstrated the value of MSAs in their reduction of claims submitted and the savings to employers (Jensen 2000, pp. 124–127).

Compared to What? The Political Economy of Medical/Health Savings Accounts

The preceding sections of this chapter have focused on the identification, viability, and economic effects of incentive-based health care plans. The major policy implication is that these consumer-directed plans, generally known as medical savings accounts, are bound to be economically feasible in reducing tax subsidies. These subsidies have distorted economic behavior, increased the role and effect of insurance beyond its financing purpose, and increased health care expenditures. Ironically, many now have less insurance and health care as a direct consequence of the subsidies that favor more insurance and more health care. Consequently, we have priced health care out of the reach of many. MSAs have fewer distortive effects, empower consumers, and release market forces to discipline adverse economic behavior. Consumers are better able to direct their scarce resources to the baskets of health care and other goods and services that are more tailored to their needs. To that extent, Mark Pauly agrees that MSAs are superior to the current employer-based insurance plans that are heavily subsidized. Certainly, MSAs are a better alternative than the previous attempt by the Clinton administration to overhaul the health care system, which Pauly described as a "heavily regulated, bizarrely subsidized arrangement" (Pauly 1994, p. 20). Pauly prefers a still better alternative in the form of closed-ended tax credit to replace tax deductibility. Under this approach, *all* tax subsidies are removed (p. 20). His argument is based on the notion that inefficient subsidies for insurance are replaced with marginal incentives to buy health insurance and medical care. This plan would provide a more efficient and equitable distribution of insurance than the current system. It would help low-income people buy health insurance and health care.

Theoretically, it appears that the Pauly proposal would do more to make our system less targeted and less distorted than would medical savings accounts. However, Pauly's proposed reform is probably not as viable as the new health savings accounts as implemented in 2004. These are heavily tax-advantaged and will allow more economizing, consumer sovereignty, and savings. Their portability feature alone will be a welcome alternative to the unreliability of employer-based insurance.

7

The Medicare Reform School

Who Pays for the Rehabilitation?

The Setting

The Medicare system in general, and its reform in 2003, may offer the best opportunity to collectively examine the most important health care policy issues in the United States. The need to accommodate market forces is paramount if we are to use markets and their incentive-stimulating price mechanisms as devices to accomplish public goals. Those goals would include access to and distribution of health care services for those who are financially and geographically disadvantaged. We know that there are no analogous mechanisms to those of markets in any other system, particularly in socialism. The connection to health care systems may be obvious. Our context is that of health care policy. While we might be tempted to contrast "Universal Health Care" or "Health Care Affordable for All" slogans with a more libertarian cry for "Free Markets," the real policy choice can be more government-controlled systems or fewer government-controlled systems. That is, do market mechanisms or price incentive aid governments that want to promote equitable outcomes? Does the United States want to broaden the population base that either can use savings or economize on its purchases to realize greater health care? Are the new health savings accounts (HSAs) in the reformed Medicare of 2003 the vehicle for this transformation?

The American government has entitled many of its elderly population to a broad range of pharmaceutical products. Simultaneously, the revised Medicare Law has established HSAs for those under sixty-five (see Chapter 6, on medical and health savings accounts). Will these changes put Americans on a savings path that will lead to greater independence and empowerment characteristic of market incentive systems? We referred in Chapter 6 to consumer-directed plans and incentive systems. The American government seems intent on increasing benefits and access to services with *strong* use of competitive market forces. The use of private insurers in the newly expanded pharmaceutical and other benefit programs is a test of the ability of market forces to keep prices affordable and choices to be those of the consumer. This has been criticized as "rents" to insurance and pharmaceutical companies. However, its purpose is the use of those who know risks to assume those risks for a fair premium. The market in the United States has become a magnet for pharmaceutical investments. The funds are flowing here as a reaction to controls in other countries. This begs the question of "what does this have to do with a government program of Medicare or any private health care provision?"

In 2003, Mark D. Whitener, deputy director of the Federal Trade Commission (FTC), in prepared remarks at the American Enterprise Institute for Public Policy Research, suggested that his perspective on the role of the private market in reform of Medicare is that "the antitrust laws have been a major factor in the development of more efficient health care markets, and in setting the stage of market-based proposals to reform Medicare" (Whitener 2003, on-line pages). Whitener suggests that the recent Medicare legislation provides choices for Medicare beneficiaries among competing health insurers. This has been and continues to be the hallmark of private markets. It is an excellent example of how government provision for health care coverage can be more efficiently provided in a competitive market than in a government-administered price, type, and amount of health care package. Anti-trust support of competitive initiatives and prosecution of anti-competitive behavior has enabled consumers to benefit. The FTC has promoted practices of physicians that had previously prevented them from extending information useful to patients. This reflects the concerns of many about the potentially harmful effects of asymmetry of information referred to in Chapter 1. The FTC has taken action to prevent blockage of innovative pricing practices of physicians (Whitener 2003, on-line pages). Market forces can play a pivotal role in promoting consumer choice, competitive pricing, and cost-effectiveness in the delivery of health care services. These markets need to be competitive. The connection to Medicare is that positive outcomes of Medicare reform require market forces to do their job. That is, our scarce health care resources can be directed to the most efficient and desired uses. The setting is clear. The positive outcomes of market mechanisms can make the delivery of health care more fairly distributed and accessible. It is a *big* test.

Other nations are using incentives in internal markets to promote the efficiency necessary to make their public programs affordable and to remain equitable. We discussed some of these initiatives in Chapters 1 and 2. As we develop this setting for Medicare reform, we sense a convergence of sorts for health care programs around the world. There is a clear impetus in the countries with controlled health systems that there should be less government regulation and, in the United States, that there should be more private market forces. The former countries have tired of inefficiency, of demand exceeding limitations of supply, and of exhausting of the government budgets (Cutler 2002, pp. 894–899). We have discussed this as a trade-off between equity and efficiency in the first two chapters.

The limitations of public budgets for health care in most countries is similar to our problems in public financing of Medicare, especially with respect to trust funds. This trust fund, as explained more carefully in the next section, has been like a digital message on a Times Square sign that says "We are keeping track of the dwindling trust funds." That is, within a short time (estimated by 2013) the fund will no longer have the ability to finance the expected benefits from current receipts. The Hospital Insurance Trust Fund is estimated to be insolvent by 2020 (Snow 2005, on-line pages). There are a number of related demographical and financial developments that do not augur well for future beneficiaries of the Medicare program.

Before the "deal was done" for the first major reform of Medicare, the Medicare Prescription Drug Improvement and Modernization Act (MMA) of 2003, at least two sides of the underlying issue were becoming evident. Indeed, before the ink dried on the new act, supporters and naysayers were acting and reacting. Beyond the political intrigue, many of the fundamental economic issues addressed in this book framed the critique of the MMA.

One of these issues is that of the involvement of market forces including competition, prices, incentives, choices, and decision making by buyers and sellers of health care services. Alan Murray called the proposal for the new act "an experiment well worth taking . . . the magic of markets is that when they work properly, they can find solutions that leave everyone better off. This is about finding ways to make the health care delivery system more efficient" (Murray 2003, on-line pages). With Medicare, we come full circle to test the proposition that systems that become more efficient *can* make it possible to afford more equity, particularly in the form of access for the poor. However, how do we handle the gaps? We know that the public funding for Medicare provides more access for the elderly. However, Medicare does, inadvertently, have certain price-excludable services. The Medicare recipients must pay an up-front deductible in order to receive hospital benefits. This one-time deductible of $876 (for 2004) paid at the beginning of each benefit period (Part A) is in addition to co-payments of $219 per day if hospital care extends beyond the sixty-day in-patient allowance to the ninetieth day of a benefit period. These payments represent serious barriers to health care for the indigent elderly population. Remember, our definition of a pure public good is that its benefits are available even to those who are unable or unwilling to pay for the good. Due to these co-payments and deductibles, the hospital benefits (Part A) of Medicare become an example of a price-excludable public good. When we begin to compile a list of the reform issues, we may see a clear reflection of the issues present in our private and public mix of health care services.

Is it possible or conceivable that retirement health care benefits would fall into the same benefit camp as Social Security, higher education, inheritance, and retirement? That is, the benefits are largely the outcomes of private savings plans that are aided and abetted by employers' contributions and government-financed tax advantages. We will temporarily leave these esoteric matters while we slink through the more mundane issues of what, how much, and when to produce health care services for Medicare beneficiaries. Who pays and who benefits? Who is excluded? Can the hospital trust fund overcome its apparent imminent demise as a financially viable mechanism? What does economic analysis reveal for us? Finally, what can we do about all of this?

The Medical System: The What?

Medicare is officially titled Health Insurance for the Aged and Disabled. It is encompassed in the Social Security Act as Title XVII. The Medicare amendments to the act in 1965 "established a health insurance program for aged persons to complement the retirement, survivors and disability insurance benefits under Title II of the Social Security Act. In addition to covering most people over the age of sixty-five, Medicare also includes Railroad Retirement disability beneficiaries, most persons with End-Stage Renal Disease (ESRD), and certain otherwise non-covered aged persons who elect to pay a premium for Medicare coverage" ("Medicare" 2003, p. 33).

Until the end of 2003, Medicare consisted of three parts: Hospital Insurance (HI) or Part A, Supplementary Medical Insurance (SMI) or Part B, and Medicare + Choice, which accepts risk contracts. By 2003, enrollment in Medicare stood at over 41 million, as compared to 19 million in 1966. In December 2003, significant provisions were added to Medicare, particularly some coverage for prescription drugs. This major reform of Medicare is titled MMA, Public Law No. 108–173.

The HI program includes coverage for in-patient hospital services, including in-patient prescription drugs, laboratory tests, X-rays, psychiatric hospitals, in-patient rehabilitation, and long-term care hospitalization when medically necessary (Annual Statistical Supplement 2003, p. 33). Skilled nursing facility (SNF) care and in-home health agency (HHA) care are also provided under HI. SNF care has to be certified as medically necessary and ordinarily has to follow hospitalization of at least three days. The SNF services are restricted to 100 days in each benefit period; for days 21 to 100, a co-payment is required. The HHA care is shared by both HI (Part A) and SMI, which is known as Part B. Hospice care is provided to terminally ill persons (life expectancy of six months or less) if they choose to accept the palliative treatments of hospice care in lieu of the regular Medicare benefits. There are a number of limitations and some co-payments required under HI. In-patient care is usually limited to ninety days during a benefit period, and co-payments are required for days sixty-one to ninety (Annual Statistical Supplement 2003, pp. 33–34).

The Supplementary Medical Insurance program (Part B) covers physician services and *some* services of chiropractors, podiatrists, dentists, optometrists, certified registered nurses, anesthetists, clinical psychologists, physician's assistants, nurse practitioners, and others. Additionally, *some* emergency room, patient clinic, ambulance, same-day surgery, laboratory tests, preventive care screening tests, ambulatory surgical center, physical therapy, occupational therapy, speech pathology, out-patient rehabilitation, kidney dialysis, and various transplant services are covered under SMI (Annual Statistical Supplement 2003, p. 34).

The financing arrangements for Part A (HI) and Part B (SMI) involve trust funds, payroll taxes, premium payments, deductibles, and co-payments. These methods of financing are sufficiently different than those for the Medical Modernization Act. We will discuss these financing techniques before turning attention to the new provisions of the MMA. In an accounting sense, the financing for Medicare is processed through separate trust funds for the Hospital Insurance (Part A) and Supplementary Medical Insurance (Part B). That is, all payments and all receipts are recorded in these trust funds. Any excess of receipts over payments in the funds are invested in U.S. Treasury Securities. The HI is mostly financed by a payroll tax on workers and their employers of 1.45 percent each for all payroll earnings. Self-employed persons pay a tax of 2.9 percent on their earnings. The HI trust fund receives additional funding from an income tax levied on a portion of Social Security benefits received by high-income individuals. Other sources of income for the HI trust fund are the general fund of the U.S. Treasury, interest income earned from the investment of excess funds, and other income (Annual Statistical Supplement 2003, p. 35).

About 25 percent of the financing for the SMI program comes from premium payments from beneficiaries who typically agree to have the monthly premium deducted from their Social Security retirement checks ($66.60 in 2004). The premium rose to $78.20 in 2005. The other 75 percent of the funding comes from the general fund of the U.S. Treasury. The costs of the program are estimated annually by a formula, which is used to determine the monthly premium. The attempt is to keep the beneficiary premium at 25 percent of the total costs. Starting in 2007, the premiums paid by beneficiaries will be adjusted to require higher premiums for some higher-income people. Specifically, beneficiaries with incomes above $80,000 for individuals and $160,000 for married couples will pay higher premiums. A sliding scale of premiums for other high-income classifications will be phased into the program from 2007 to 2010 (MMA Summary 2004, on-line pages).

Medicare + Choice (Part C) is a set of options that allows beneficiaries to choose private plans that have accepted contracts from the government. These contracts must meet financial and service prerequisites. The private plans must contain the provisions of the current Medicare benefits as a minimum requirement. These plans may include additional services. If the plans receive payments in excess of their costs, they must return the excess payments or provide additional services. There are two types of plans under Medicare + Choice. One is a "risk" contract. That is, managed care organizations (MCOs), including health maintenance organizations (HMOs) and preferred provider organizations (PPOs), offer coordinated care plans that guarantee services at the terms of the contract. The risk undertaken by these organizations is that the escalating costs of health care may surpass the agreed amount of payment under the contract. Any cost differences would have to be absorbed by the MCO. The other option under Medicare + Choice is that of private, unrestricted fee-for-service (FFS) plans. These plans allow the Medicare beneficiaries to choose from among providers who have agreed to payment and condition terms. This option is *not* a risk contract for the private providers (Annual Statistical Supplement 2003, pp. 35–36). Under the Medicare Modernization Act of 2003, Medicare Advantage (MA) replaced Medicare + Choice under Part C of Medicare. The MMA calls for plans that are designed to foster regional competition through Federally Qualified Health Centers (FQHCs). Analysis of the regional competition will evaluate "whether direct competition between the private plans and the original Medical fee-for-service program will enhance competition in Medicare" (MMA Summary 2004, on-line pages). The Medicare Advantage plans provide beneficiaries with more health care choices as part of the Medicare program. These choices include *managed care plans* that are similar to the network plans offered by employers for their employees' PPOs, *private* FFS plans, and *specialty plans* that are designed to provide focused care to treat people with specific medical conditions. These specialty plans are, in effect, disease management plans (U.S. Department of Health and Human Services [hereafter U.S. DHS] 2005, pp. 53–55). These choices and the redirection of resources to preventive care and disease management address some of the fundamental issues in health care delivery. Not only will the resources being used be more efficacious in health care outcomes but also they are more likely to be cost effective. Other changes in the revised Medicare program, particularly in the coverage of pharmaceutical products, will be discussed in the next section.

These three parts of Medicare do not cover all health care services. Medicare does not cover long-term nursing care, custodial care, dentures and dental care, eyeglasses, or hearing aids. For services not covered by the Medicare program, and for deductibles and co-payments, the beneficiaries are responsible for the costs. As alluded to earlier in this chapter, those payments can act as barriers to care for the poor. For Hospital Insurance there is a deductible ($876 for 2004) charged for each beneficiary *before* the benefits of hospital care can be realized. This deductible is the beneficiary's share of hospital costs for the first sixty days of a benefit period. An additional co-payment per day ($219 in 2004) is charged to the beneficiary through the ninetieth day of a benefit period. For skilled nursing care, the beneficiaries under HI are charged a co-payment ($109.50 in 2004) per day. Other sources of financing come through the annual deductible, the monthly premiums, and co-insurance payments for the services received (Annual Statistical Supplement 2003, pp. 34–36).

One of the major issues of this book is the separation of the consumer from the provider with respect to the terms of exchange (price, quantity, availability, type of payment). In a world of volume purchasing and pre-established contracts, we have forms of this separation in many health care and non–health care markets. However, in health care markets, we have unique features that compound the separation between buyer and seller, including asymmetry of information and a complex interrelationship among government, institutional, and market forces. When a government agency enters into a nonrisk contract with a private insurance carrier, the terms of exchange for the consumer become constrained by the "one-size-fits-all" approach to health care. The differences in choices for price, quantity, and availability of health care become obvious whenever government enters into contracts that carry risks for MCOs, PPOs, and HMOs. In these contracts, the private organization sets the premium charged to the government at a level that reflects actual risk, administrative costs, and profits/surpluses. Implicitly, the premium also considers the discounted prices that providers will accept and the prices that employers and employees will be willing to pay. Thus, the separation between sellers and buyers of health care is reduced. The redirection of health care services to that of consumers and providers is enhanced with the risk contracts. Consumer-directed health care services are more manifest in health savings accounts, Medigap policies, and associations of buyers where consumers make more individual choices. As indicated earlier, the buyers and sellers of health care services become separated in Medicare since a wide range of services are not provided. Yet, the consumer takes a package of health care services that includes some items of little interest and excludes some items of great interest and use. All of this is preliminary to an analysis of reform issues later in this chapter. Before looking at the reform issues, we now take a look at the most recent reform of Medicare, the Medicare Prescription Drug Improvement and Modernization Act of 2003.

The MMA partially fills one of the gaps in Medicare, that is, a lack of coverage of needed health care services. The absence of coverage for senior citizens of pharmaceutical prescription drugs outside of hospitals stays has been a major social and political concern for some years. Some people wondered why one of the most important and expensive health care needs did not fall under the purview of Medicare. The MMA also contains some coverage that reflects issues of increasing concern and importance. The MMA includes disease management (DM) programs. These include demonstration programs for health care quality, chronic care improvement programs, coordination of medication therapy with disease management programs, and others.

The key feature of the MMA is the voluntary prescription drug benefit program. The inclusion of prescription drug benefits is the most significant change in the history of the Medicare program. The benefits have been phased in between the temporary Medicare-approved drug discount plan (2004 through 2005) and the Medicare prescription drug plans that are scheduled to begin on January 1, 2006 (U.S. DHS 2005, pp. 7–15). The federal government touts the new program as one that offers "eligible Medicare beneficiaries, regardless of income or health status, access to more coverage options, options which provide enhanced benefits, with cost-sharing, additional beneficiary protections and assistance, such as access to negotiated prices, catastrophic coverage limits, and premium subsidies for certain low-income beneficiaries" (MMA Summary 2004, on-line pages). This new drug program is offered through both the new Part C, Medicare Advantage (MA) program (replaces Medicare + Choice), which adds prescription drug benefits to the coverage for the special needs of some individuals in a disease management plan, and a new, stand-alone Part D Prescription Drug Plan (PDP). The new PDP is the flagship for the reform of Medicare. This prescription drug program relies heavily on the use of private plans to not only provide coverage but also to bear some of the financial risks for drug costs (MMA Summary 2004, on-line pages). This combination of government provision of a good that is privately produced is the hallmark of a system that is conscious of the need (normative judgment) for health care services and seeks the most efficient (positive analysis) means of satisfying that need. Can market forces prompt risk sharing or risk assumption through competitive institutions? Is it possible that these market forces can create an environment for lower costs for an increasing array of pharmaceutical products?

The first step in the transition to Medicare coverage of pharmaceutical benefits is the use of Medicare-approved discount cards. The cards were a temporary (May 2004–December 2005) program designed to get everyone ready for the prescription drug plans in 2006. The discount cards were provided to all Medicare beneficiaries except those who have outpatient benefits under Medicaid. Medicare arranged for private companies to offer Medicare-approved discount cards. Companies that offer the discount cards are limited to charging no more than thirty dollars per year for enrollment. The card entitles the beneficiary to the use of a designated list of approved pharmacies for that card. Each beneficiary can use only one Medicare-approved discount card at a time. Non-Medicare-approved discount cards can be used along with the Medicare-approved card but not for the same prescription at the same time. Some low-income people (earning up to $12,569 per year for individuals and up to $16,862 a year for married couples) become eligible for a credit of $600 in 2004 toward their discount card (U.S. DHS 2005, pp. 7–12).

The Medicare Prescription Drug Plans under Part D were scheduled to begin on January 1, 2006. These plans allow beneficiaries a choice of standard coverage or alternative coverage of actuarially equivalent benefits. Both of these plans have access to negotiated markets for drug prices (MMA Summary 2004, on-line pages). The PDPs have the following features:

1. a monthly premium (approximately $35 per month);
2. a $250 per year deductible;
3. a payment of 25 percent of each year's drug costs from $251 to $2,250; the plan pays the other 75 percent;
4. the beneficiaries pay 100 percent of each year's drug cost from $2,251 up to a cap of $3,600 on out-of-pocket costs;
5. beneficiaries pay 5 percent of each year's drug costs over $3,600; the plan pays the other 95 percent (U.S. DHS 2005, p. 140).

The plans will vary from this general scheme, but the concept of risk and cost sharing is the same. These prescription drug plans parallel many of the other features of the MMA, including choice, risk assumption, sharing of costs with deductibles and out-of-pocket expenses, and coverage for those very high catastrophic costs of health care. Full coverage at government expense would be prohibitively expensive and allocatively inefficient. The cost-sharing provisions allow more choice for individuals on how they allocate their income over a wide range of goods and services. The plans bring seller or provider and buyer or consumer closer together on the critical questions of how, how much, what, when, and for whom to provide health care services. The plans would avoid the "one-size-fits-all" government packages. The prescription drug plan also allows special assistance to low-income individuals. Eligible individu-

als would have incomes below 135 percent of the poverty line with resources not more than three times the maximum resources to qualify for
the Supplementary Security Income (SSI) program. These individuals
would be entitled to a premium subsidy of 100 percent of the premium
of the low-income benchmark. There is a detailed plan that establishes a
sliding-scale premium subsidy for other eligible low-income individuals. Other provisions include cost sharing for generic and other drugs of
one to two dollars for income groups below the poverty line beginning
in 2007 (MMA Summary 2004, on-line pages). The MMA establishes
procedures and a State Pharmaceutical Assistance Transition Commission to address the need for coordination of the various state programs
with the federal program (MMA Summary 2004, on-line pages).

Even though the prescription drug benefits represent the major part
of the MMA, a number of key provisions in the act reveal its comprehensive reform nature and indicate its reliance on market forces. A summary of these provisions follows:

1. *Preventive services.* The MMA authorizes coverage for an initial
preventive physical examination, cardiovascular screening blood tests,
and screening tests for diabetes.

2. *Cost controls.* For Medicare Part B out-patient biological drugs,
the controls would limit the prices to 95 percent of the average whole-
sale price. Other out-patient drugs would be held at the average price for
the competitive acquisition areas. For ambulatory surgery centers (ASCs),
the consumer price index (CPI) will be adjusted downward to correct
for biases.

3. *Evaluation of the need for payment.* This is assessed under Part B
of Medicare for certain services by professionals, such as a certified
registered nurse who provides surgical first assisting services, clinical
staff of thoracic and cardiac surgeons, and vision rehabilitation professionals. Any revisions in payment would almost certainly require changes
in the relative value scale used in the determination of reimbursements
for physicians who render services to Medicare beneficiaries.

4. *Demonstration projects.* Many of these focus on quality of care
provided for patients with chronic conditions. Some of these demon-
strations will test the value of consumer-directed care. Others will place
quality of care in the context of disease management programs.

5. *Clinical effectiveness.* Much of this emphasis is related to the previously mentioned interest in quality of care and its efficiency. The re-

search called for in the MMA is to provide some empirical evidence of the "outcomes, comparative clinical effectiveness, and appropriateness of health care items and services; and strategies for improving the efficiency of such programs" (MMA Summary 2004, on-line pages).

6. *Citizen's Health Care Working Group.* This group could be an effective force for consumer-directed care. Its technique would be to hold hearings to examine a number of issues including the capacities of the public and private health care systems to provide for increased coverage, the costs of health care, and the enrollment of eligible beneficiaries in available public and private settings. Most importantly, Section 1014 in the MMA calls for "the role of *evidence-based medical practices* that can be documented as restoring, maintaining, or improving a patient's health and the use of technology in supporting providers in improving quality of care and lowering costs" (MMA Summary 2004, Section 1014, on-line pages).

7. *Importation of prescription drugs.* Section 1121 of the MMA allows pharmacists and wholesalers to import prescription drugs from Canada. Prerequisites include qualified laboratory drug testing and labeling as well as registration of the imported prescription drugs by the Canadian sellers with United States officials. Additionally, the drugs must come from a licensed pharmacy with a valid prescription to be issued in final dosage form from a registered manufacturer. The dosage is limited to personal use for a maximum of ninety days. Also, the U.S. Secretary of Health and Human Services can determine other conditions in order to maintain public safety (MMA Summary 2004, on-line pages).

8. *Health savings accounts (HSAs).* These accounts are combined with high-deductible health plans (HDHPs) for individuals under the age of sixty-five. They are a fundamental part of a major redirection of health care in favor of ownership accounts and greater consumer choice. HSAs are covered in Chapter 6. Although HSAs are designed as stand-alone portable individual accounts, they may be offered by employers under their cafeteria-style plans (MMA Summary 2004, on-line pages).

The Issues for Reform

The Medicare Prescription Drug Improvement and Modernization Act of 2003 provided needed reform in our nation's health care system. The MMA addresses, or at best, puts into proper perspective the many issues of reform, particularly those that appear to be in need of greater

Figure 7.1   **Medicare Outlays vs. Medicare Tax Receipts and Premiums**

Outlays in trillions of dollars

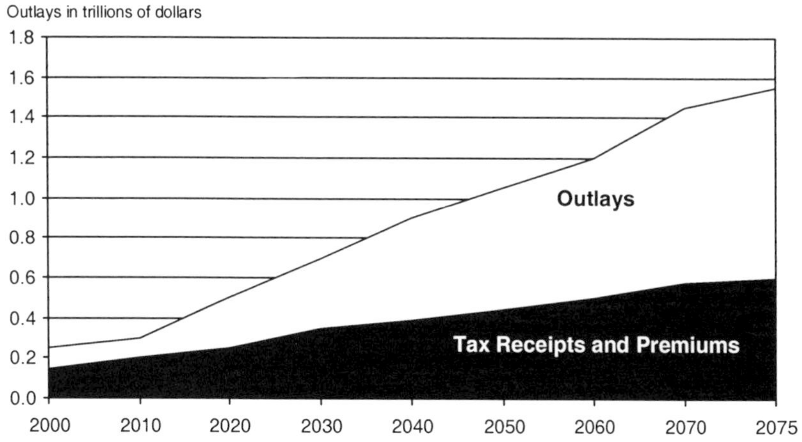

Source: Annual Report of the Board of Trustees of the Federal Hospital Insurance and Supplemental Medical Insurance Trust Funds. Available at www.whitehouse.gov.2005.

Note: Outlays include Part A and Part B outlays in constant 2000 dollars. Tax receipts and premiums are defined as payroll tax, tax on Social Security benefits, and Part B premiums in constant 2000 dollars.

involvement of market forces. These market forces are now more likely to be consumer-directed and to be responsive to quality measures, particularly with respect to clinical effectiveness teamed with disease management. While the focus of the MMA was clearly that of coverage for pharmaceutical drugs, the act was quite comprehensive in regard to the preceding issues. The role of government in providing, if not producing, health care services for the senior population is tempered by the need for an efficient and desired system of market demand in the allocation of scare resources. We can express our wishes for more kidney dialysis, pharmaceutical drugs, or heart bypass surgery more effectively with private goods.

However, many important issues of Medicare reform remain. Most of them are financial and economic issues. Among the financial reasons for reform is the need for solvency. The Medicare system is clearly headed for financial collapse. As Figure 7.1 indicates, the outlays of the two trust funds for Part A and Part B of Medicare will greatly exceed the receipts of payroll taxes, tax on Social Security benefits, and Part B premiums.

Figure 7.2 **The Aging of Society Makes Reform Urgent**

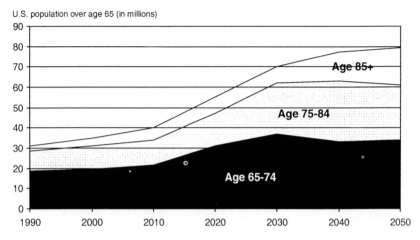

Source: U.S. Bureau of the Census (1995).

This financing gap was $51 billion in 2000 and is projected to be $216 billion in 2020 and $368 billion in 2030 (all of these figures are in constant 2000 dollars) ("A Blueprint for New Beginnings" 2004 on-line pages). Recent reports from Washington indicate that payments from the trust fund will exceed receipts by 2017. The Social Security trustees have projected insolvency in 2041. The major sources of this problem have been rising health care costs and the aging of the population. This aging problem is illustrated in Figure 7.2 and is a function of demographic factors that have been building for many years and will continue to manifest themselves over a period of forty or more years.

In the period of 2010 to 2030, the population over the age of sixty-five will increase from 39.7 million to 69.1 million. Life expectancy is projected to reach the age of seventy-six for people born in 2000. More people are living beyond the age of eighty-five and even the age of one hundred. This, coupled with seniors having more health care services available and using them more regularly, has had a major effect on rising health care expenditures. Consequently, the ratio of workers to beneficiaries paying Medicare payroll taxes (Part A of Medicare) and premiums for Part B of Medicare to the number of Medicare beneficiaries was approximately one to four in 2004. It is estimated that this ratio will fall to just over one to two in 2030 to just one to two in 2070. In other words, each worker will have to pay more

Table 7.1

Current Medicare and Sample Federal Employee Cost-Sharing Requirements for In-patient Hospital Care

	Participant pays	
Hospital stay	Current Medicare	Standard Blue Cross/Blue Shield plan for federal employees
Days 1–60	$840 per admission	$100 co-payment per admission
Days 61–90	$210 per day	$0 per day
Days 91–150	$420 per day	$0 per day
Over 150 Days	All costs	$0 per day

Source: U.S. Treasury (2003).

in payroll taxes in the future or benefits will have to be reduced ("A Blueprint for New Beginnings" 2004, on-line pages). Part of this problem has been addressed in the MMA. As noted earlier in this chapter, premiums paid into the trust fund for Part B will be scaled so that some higher-income individuals will pay proportionally more than lower-income individuals.

Another financial issue is that Medicare covers only about 43 percent of beneficiaries' medical expenses. This is reflected in the fact that over 80 percent of Medicare beneficiaries opt to buy private Medigap policies. Some of this gap will be filled by the new pharmaceutical benefit program, particularly when it goes into full force. Preventive services have been largely inadequate, although they have been expanded, at least for an initial screening process, under reform enacted in the MMA ("A Blueprint for New Beginnings" 2004, on-line pages).

The payment of deductibles and co-payments by Medicare beneficiaries, particularly for hospital in-patient services, under Part A has been a burden and, sometimes, a barrier to necessary health care services. As indicated earlier in this chapter, Medicare Part A beneficiaries must pay an up-front amount of $840 for each hospital admission. This covers care for the first sixty days of hospitalization. The next segment of care requires still higher co-payments for extended days of 91 to 150 days with all costs paid by the patient for stays over 150 days. Those payments are particularly difficult for low-income seniors. These payments are in sharp contrast to the federal employee cost-sharing requirements for hospital care (U.S. Treasury 2003, on-line pages). Table 7.1 illustrates this contrast.

Figure 7.3 **Percentage of Medicare Beneficiaries with Drug Coverage, by Source of Coverage** (2002 projection)

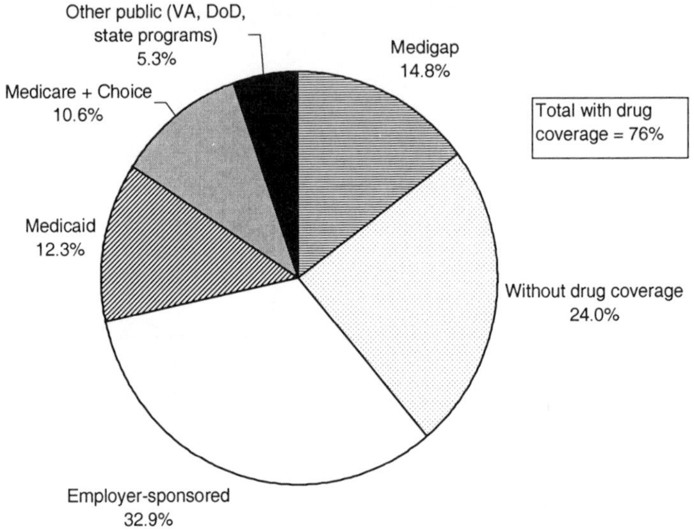

Source: Centers for Medicare and Medicaid Services (CMS) 2001, http://cms.hhs.gov.

A related issue is the extent to which the inclusion of pharmaceutical drug coverage in the MMA is necessary, extends coverage to needed groups, and/or is injurious to the risk pools and, hence, premiums of the standard comprehensive employer-based insurance policies. This issue is, in turn, related to retirees' wealth portfolios and recent court actions by employers to deny health coverage promised to retirees. Over 32 percent of Medicare beneficiaries in 2002 had employer-sponsored health insurance with drug coverage. As the chart in Figure 7.3 indicates, about 76 percent of Medicare beneficiaries had drug coverage in 2002. Only 24 percent were without any drug coverage.

Figure 7.3 shows that government programs, excluding the MMA of 2003, covered 28 percent of the beneficiaries through Medicare + Choice, Medicaid, and other public programs. Some would question why the taxpayers are asked to support a senior pharmaceutical drug program for all seniors rather than for those who lack coverage for drugs. There is some special assistance in the MMA for seniors who are in the ranges of below 100 percent of the poverty line as well as at 135 and 150 percent of the poverty line. The details of this coverage are discussed in the previous section of this chapter. We do know that the consumer price index for the elderly (CPI-E) has usually been at a higher level than the consumer price index for wage earners. A 0.38 percent average higher annual rate for the CPI-E is attributable to the greater amount of medical care expenditures for seniors than for others (Hobijn and Lagakos 2003, on-line pages). Even though people over sixty-five spend more per capita on health care than people under sixty-five, the rates among the younger population are rapidly growing. According to research done by Kenneth Thorpe of Emory University, per capita spending for people in the over-sixty-five age brackets in 2000 was generally in the $5,000 to $6,000 range. The fifty-to-sixty-four age group was in the $3,000-plus range. Lower per capita spending was reported for younger groups. Quite a different story was reported for the *percent change* in per capital spending from 1987 to 2000. The ages of thirty to thirty-nine had an over 80 percent change in per capita spending. The increase for the forty to sixty-four age groups was over 70 percent. This is in contrast to an *under* 60 percent change in per capita spending for ages sixty-five to eighty. Those over the age of eighty had only a 29 percent change in per capita spending in the same period of time. These numbers do not augur well for the fiscal soundness of Medicare. Many of these younger groups, according to the research, are experiencing an increase in chronic diseases and disability. Many of these afflictions are related to the rise in obesity in younger people. The cost of treating this new trend of illness is expected to manifest itself in increased hospital spending when the now-young become Medicare beneficiaries (Wysocki 2003, on-line pages).

The financial solvency of the Medicare trust funds depends in part on the relationship among health status, life expectancy, and health care expenditures of the elderly. A study done by James Lubitz, Liming Cai, Ellen Kramarow, and Harold Lentzner found that a person aged seventy without any functional limitations had a life expectancy of 14.3 years and expected health care expenditures of about $136,000. This was compared to a person with some functional limitations at age seventy who would have a life expectancy of only 11.6 years but would be expected to have cumulative expenditures of about $145,000. Higher expenditures and lower life expectancy were reported for institutionalized persons. This study supports the notion that reform measures directed at the population *under* the age of sixty-five may improve the health status and life-expectancy levels of the elderly over time. Based on the study, this effort could be accomplished without increasing health care spending (Lubitz et al. 2003, p. 1048).

Increases in Medicare's spending may raise issues about distributional questions. Does the Medicare program have greater transfers to some groups than might be expected by the payments into the system? Mark McClellan and Jonathan Skinner (1999) ask the question, "Who pays and who benefits?" in the Medicare system. They find that along with the impending crisis in solvency for the trust fund, there are these distributional questions. The authors found that net dollar transfers were greater for wealthier beneficiaries, that is, benefits over a lifetime actually were highly correlated with income levels. The reform measures suggested by the authors include some already in progress. For example, Part B higher-income beneficiaries are scheduled to pay higher premiums than lower-income beneficiaries starting in 2007, as discussed earlier in this chapter. The authors suggest adding an ambulatory prescription drug benefit and long-term care benefits combined with fewer benefits for acute care hospital services. They also suggest more coverage for those disease categories that have a greater incidence in lower-income populations. This would include substance abuse and some advanced conditions of diabetes. A more fundamental reform would be to change the Medicare system to that of a defined premium for a choice of approved insurance plans. If the premiums were risk-adjusted by health status, there might be a correction for the imbalance of transfer payments that currently favors higher-income beneficiaries. The authors also favor Medicare accounts that would allow workers to pay in advanced for their own retirement health benefits. McClellan and Skinner's 1999 article presages the health savings accounts for people under sixty-five in the Medicare Modernization Act passed in 2003 (McClellan and Skinner 1999, on-line pages).

Another Medicare reform issue centers on geographic variation in Medicare spending; specifically, "in some regions of the United States, Medicare pays more than twice as much per person for health care as it pays in other regions . . . Fee-For-Service (FFS) Medicare in the Miami Hospital referral region in 1996 was $8,414 . . . [and] $3,341 . . . in the Minneapolis region" (Wennberg, Fisher, and Skinner 2002, web exclusive, p. W96). The variations among regions was attributable to the availability and use of "supply-sensitive services" identified as physician visits, specialists as consultants, and the extent of hospitalization. The study finds "strong associations between higher spending and greater use of supply-sensitive care" (p. W102), as described earlier. Further, this higher spending did not necessarily result in more effective care. The study suggests that Medicare reform should be "based on the principles of shared decision making and the promotion of centers of medical decision making" (p. W96).

Conclusions and Policy Implications

Much of what has been accomplished in Medicare reform, as well as the measures suggested by many for additional reforms, depends on the knowledge, understanding, and appreciation of the relative roles of government, institutions, and market forces. The institutional role of providers and professionals centers on the issues of quality, clinical effectiveness, and disease management. The institutions of health care delivery bear the responsibility, if not the obligation, to develop standards of excellence and to establish mechanisms to monitor and coordinate their professional colleagues in this effort. The market should be the enabling force in determining the values of health care services. This should allow the consumers to be willing to pay prices for Medicare and other health care services that reflect their tastes and preferences. These prices should reflect the implicit and explicit costs of the supplier. The patient and the provider should be directly involved in the medical decision making. The patient depends on the professional, not a third party, to make an informed decision. Both the patient and the physician want an effective outcome. The market would allow the consumer to have more choices in health care and for the consumer to determine the basket of health care services. In a consumer-directed health care system, the consumer rejects a basket of health care services that is a one-size-fits-all plan, usually of government origin.

The government, in this ideal world, provides the vehicles for quality health care that promote professional, clinically effective care and consumer choices. The government can create an atmosphere, guided by favorable tax policies, that encourages ownership of accounts that promote saving for future retirement needs. It appears that we have begun to travel this path with the enactment of the MMA of 2003. There still remain many issues of equity, access, insurance coverage, and distributional and geographical inequalities. The government must also be vigorous in keeping the health care market competitive in an atmosphere of market-based proposals. In this regard, anti-trust laws and their enforcement can be effective against restraints on competition. These restraints are significant as Medicare reform requires competitive private insurance markets. The success of the new pharmaceutical drug coverage in the MMA depends on a competitive insurance industry. Market forces can work well, but they need to be competitive in order to have gains in efficient outcomes for all.

8

Conclusions and Policy Implications

Fantasy and Reality: First Believe and Then Get Real!

The issues discussed in this book illustrate both the dimensions of the underlying issues in health care policy and the complexities involved in the pursuit of solutions. As in most controversial issues, there are extreme views as well as more moderate ones. At one end of the political spectrum is the banner of either "universal health care" or "affordable health care for all." At the other end of the political spectrum are the consumer-directed or patient power dicta of those who are enamored of market mechanisms. The universal health care advocates would centralize all health care decisions and financing in the hands of a government single buyer and budget agency. There would be no need for private health insurance. Indeed, spending one's own resources to gain more access more quickly would be banned under the more extreme versions of the single-buyer, global budget plans. Under the consumer-related schemes, there would be less government and the major roles would be assumed by consumers and the medical profession. Government would enable "ownership" of one's resources so that individuals would be empowered to make their own decisions based on their preferences, but constrained by their budgets. Private insurance companies would be the risk assumers (for a price or premium). In competitive markets, buyers and sellers of health care services and health insurance would make exchanges that increase well-being. The global budget plans would emphasize access and equitable distribution. The consumer-directed market incentives plans would emphasize efficiency and increases in the health services that consumers need and want.

Both of these extremes imply rationing of health care services. The more extreme the plan, the more extreme the trade-offs or rationing. One extreme would place limits on the types, amounts, and availability of services. The other would place limits on access to the health care system, particularly for the uninsured and the low-income people. People would have to be true believers, actual facts not withstanding, to accept either of the two extreme positions. In the United States, we have seen politicization of major issues. In academic settings, faculty have become advocates of universal health care and often energize students to write, speak, carry banners, and form political action groups in support of their cause. Those on the side of consumer-directed market decisions sometimes become almost libertarian in their denial of strong, if any, roles for government. Government can, of course, release market forces through changes in the tax code.

These are the fantasies of the left and the right. On the left, would it not be great if the government took care of all our health care needs? Government could remove the markets or financial institutions from any influence. There would be affordable health care for all. On the right, would it not be great if government influence disappeared and all of us could direct markets to our own choices of health care? Our menus for health care and how much we want to pay could be much more favorable to most of us than the government-administered prices and formulary-approved menu. Often, the supporters of these polarized solutions are closely aligned with a political party or splinter groups. At a rally for universal health care, supporters are often joined by other groups on the left side of political action, such as advocates for a living wage, Health Care Task Group, Americans for Health Care, and peace and justice groups. On the right side, employers, representatives of medical groups, insurance companies, pharmaceutical firms, and managed care organizations would join forces with political parties interested in using competitive market forces.

The extreme positions have had the effect of crowding out the more viable options for public policy that reside comfortably in the middle in both political and economic terms. In this book, we have searched for solutions containing a mix of public and private financing of health care that recognizes health care as a public good and allows some private financing. The private funding serves both as an extension of health care goods and services beyond the limits of public budgets and as a substitute for public funding when more efficiency is warranted.

The fantasy about health care lives in the hearts of the true believers on the left and right extremes of the political spectrum. We say, believe if you are so inclined. However, to accomplish significant reform for the issues concerning health care, we need to get real! The reality is in the mix of public and private funding, including the inherent trade-offs and the implicit rationing in *all* of the proposed solutions. The economic reality is that every proposed solution has a trade-off. The economist is obliged to say, "You can do it that way, but I will tell you what it will cost." The costs are often implicit in the form of opportunity costs. The United States has decided to partially cover the costs of pharmaceutical drugs for the elderly. However, beneficiaries will be restricted in their choices to those in the government-administered formulary. In order to develop a set of policy implications or designs, we will summarize what we have learned or known from this excursion into health care issues. We will conclude this chapter and the book with "lessons for reform."

What Do We Know? What Have We Learned?

1. *The trade-offs.* In Chapters 1 and 2, we learned that as public funding of health care expenditures increases, the percentage of gross domestic product devoted to health care expenditures decreases. In general, we infer that public budgets have a more constraining effect than do private budgets. We do know that there are other factors that contribute to this otherwise simple trade-off. In the United States, we have the presence of third-party payers, including managed care organizations, insurance firms, and government, that finance and subsidize the provision of health care. These third-party payers act to reduce the usual budget constraints of consumer income and prices of health care goods and services. Therefore, consumers who want to maximize their utility (satisfaction) in the absence of inhibiting budget limits will spend more on health care than if normal constraints were in place. This understanding leads us to some of the more serious implications of the trade-offs related to public funding of health care expenditures.

2. *Rationing of health care.* One effect of reliance on public funding is that of rationing. We learned about rationing in our exploration of health care issues. In the United Kingdom, the National Health Service has established limits on the availability of kidney dialysis through its rationing of the limited number of facilities and personnel. With demand for kidney dialysis far exceeding this limited supply, the services are rationed primarily on the basis of age. People over the age of seventy-five are effectively

denied care. Some form of rationing takes place in the short run when supply cannot fully adjust to changes in demand. In a market setting, the relatively scarce goods and services and the resources used in their production are priced higher than the relatively abundant goods and services. Given the presence of competitive markets and sufficient information, consumers and business firms will economize on the use of the more expensive (scarce) goods/services and resources. Conversely, the lower-priced services (abundant) will increase in attractiveness. As the relatively scarce services and resources are used more frequently, their prices will rise. The price mechanisms do the rationing. The highest bidders get the scarce goods. Over the long run, you might expect the supply of scarce goods and services to increase to meet the demand. The societal trade-off is that some needed health care services are denied to those who cannot afford or are unwilling to pay for them, at least in the short run. However, the market can and has responded to increases in demand for more health care services in quantity, type, and availability.

3. *Why an understanding of the extremes is important to the issue of rationing.* We have learned that the universal health care advocates desire a sufficient quantity of health care services that would be accessible and affordable for all. This is an extreme position that ignores most of the economic and political realities. In 1994, Tennessee enacted a new program to finance health care called TennCare, which was publicized as a lower-cost plan that would accommodate larger numbers of the medically uninsured. The government would manage competition and produce savings through volume purchasing and subsidies for preventive care programs. The program extended enrollment to those who were not eligible for Medicaid. The enrollment included some who are in the over $100,000 levels of income and covers over 20 percent of the state's population. TennCare now comprises close to one-third of the state budget of Tennessee. Talk about health care for all! Virtually all costs for prescribed drugs, even aspirin and antacids, are covered. Prescription drug costs increased by over 20 percent in 2003. As we identified the political mood described earlier, activists have fought denials of claims by the constituent managed care organizations that provide insurance and program administration. Legal costs for Tennessee are as high as $1,600 per case. The governor of Tennessee is considering a termination of TennCare. Some managed care organizations have been in receivership. The state has taken on most of the premium and risk functions ("Hillary Care in Tennessee" 2004, p. A14).

This leaves us with two messages. One is that the believers—a.k.a. the activists—are certainly looking at and advocating for more access to the health care system. The other message is that these extreme positions are simply not economically viable. On the political side, public budgets cannot afford the generosity. Consequently, other state needs, such as education, become impoverished. This extreme position on the left does, in effect, give us a sense of an unbridled and undisciplined demand for health care, as if it were a "free good." Health care services and products are *not* free. There are large trade-offs in denial of alternative public goods or less consumption of public goods. Tax increases to support these programs distort prices and allocate our scare resources to less efficient and desired uses. On the other hand, there are those who would leave most health care choices to the dictates of the physician and the preferences of consumers that are implicit in the demand for health care. Given the advances of medical technology, if consumers and their physicians want more kidney dialysis, pharmaceutical drugs, open-heart surgery, and less invasive forms of medical procedures, there will be a clear market signal and an expected response. This position is considered to be extreme by some. However, there is evidence that markets are responsive to incentives. Indeed, price controls on pharmaceutical drugs have been associated with potential decreases in innovation in research and development. One recent study in *Health Economics* estimates that if the United States were to allow the reimportation of drugs from Europe, there would be significant decreases in research for new drugs in the United States (Vernon 2005, pp. 1–16). The converse has taken place. In recent years, we have witnessed increased flows of investment from Europe into pharmaceutical research in the United States. Markets are responsible. However, markets do fail at times and may effectively exclude those who are unwilling or unable to pay. There are rents extracted from the market by some for-profit hospital groups who can administer prices and ignore the competitive efforts of managed care (see Chapter 4).

Those who advocate either the "single-buyer global budget affordable health care for all" approach or the "consumer-directed market incentives individual choice" teach us that we need a private-public mix of financing and delivery of health care systems. We need to be efficient and responsive to the differing needs of medical providers and their patients (consumers). Also, we need to recognize the need for government to provide, at least, the safety net. This is to have mechanisms in place to assure minimal access, financial and physical, to health care services.

Each of the extreme positions has its limits. Concern only for having an efficient system tends to ignore the needs of low-income people. Concern only for affordable care for all ignores the reality of public budget limits. Hence, rationing will occur either by limiting quality and availability of health care or by limiting care to those who can afford it.

4. *Reality between the extremes: a search for the "middle" solutions.* We learned some tough lessons on public funding versus private funding. Are they substitutes for each other or complements? Under current schemes, there is considerable resistance to the extension of public funding for Medicaid since the federal, state, and local/regional budgets for the program have been crowding out other needs. In New York State, Medicaid accounts for over 40 percent of the entire budget. Counties in New York have witnessed increased health costs and increases in enrollment for Medicaid. The choices are clear. Either increase the tax revenues or place controls on the amounts expended. Neither of these options is politically popular. Alternatively, counties have asked state legislatures to assume more of the costs. Similarly, states have asked the federal government to finance a large share of their budgets for Medicaid. Enter the notion of the federal government giving the states block grants or a fixed amount to run their own Medicaid services. This idea is akin to the largely successfully welfare reform (1996) program. As with welfare, block grants to the states would end the entitlement status based on enrollment and any changes in health care costs (Hernandez and Baker 2005, pp. N 23, N28).

Regardless of what the political pundits wish to call these proposals, the result is some form of rationing. The federal government would say, "Here is a fixed grant of 30 billion dollars to New York State to spend as it sees fit for health care services for the poor." The state could say that the distribution would be to divide the lump sum among the eligible Medicaid population. This is a similar design to that proposed by Governor Jeb Bush of Florida. If given a waiver from the federal government (how about it, brother?), a revenue cap would be placed on state expenditures. The resultant state revenue would be distributed equally (with some adjustments for those at higher illness risk) among the state's Medicaid beneficiaries. In the Florida case, the Medicaid beneficiaries would be given the premium amount necessary to buy private insurance. What had been a blank check for Medicaid beneficiaries to cash for "entitled" escalating costs of health care becomes a fixed amount of cash (premium or voucher) to spend on one's own (empowered) choice of health care needs. A government grant plus private empowerment to spend is a private-public plan. This sort of mixed system is an example of what is ignored or disavowed by those on the opposite poles of political beliefs. We give little or no credit to our intellect when we reject, out of hand, the *other* party's proposal, particularly when the other party is in political power.

This discourse is especially useful when we examine the predilections and presumptions underlying political histories and directions of different countries. Historically, with some important recent changes to the contrary, we have presumed, in America, that the Jeffersonian image of individualism and pluralism represented in free political and economic institutions would be the model for anyone to challenge in the quest for social change. Thomas Jefferson believed in a limited role for government. It should not be surprising that over 200 years after President Jefferson's inaugural message, the state continues to use markets and private financing for over 50 percent of health care expenditures. Most of the nation's hospitals are operated as not-for-profit *private* corporations. And yet, the United States has the highest percentage of gross domestic product (GDP) devoted to health care expenditures of all the industralized countries. Recently, political paradigms in the United States have been changing. The second George W. Bush term of office continued the notion that in order to have *more private* "ownership accounts" or health savings accounts (HSAs), there needed to be *more* public support. This is in the form of tax code changes, which essentially leave accumulated amounts and any earned interest tax-free. Combined with the involvement of major insurance and financial institutions in the private sector, HSAs represent individuals pursuing their own menus for health care with the aid of employers and government. This is another public-private plan with a twist of government incentives. Most other industrial nations have been more progressive: Government-directed activity, social pensions, welfare systems, and health care have been part of the political, labor, and social fabric for some time. These other nations generally guide their health systems to more equitable outcomes for the population. This is their presumed approach. This emphasis has caused anxiety and some political turmoil as public costs of health care and social welfare systems have increased taxes and the costs of doing business. Even so, these nations have much lower percentages of GDP devoted to health care expenditures than the United States and much higher percentages of health care that are publicly funded. The predilection is still to tap the public purse. This direction is not without some difficulties. As these nations exhaust their public funds, they seek *more* financing from private sources to allow the excess demand to be met.

Studies cited in the book found that:

1. Increases in public funding relative to private funding were associated with higher mortality rates. Since government budgets were limited, some patients were denied the needed drug therapy or were delayed in their access to it. Therefore, we saw lower survival rates in some European countries as compared with the United States, where markets functioned to demand the therapy (Cutler 2002, pp. 881-906).

2. Increases in public funding relative to changes in private funding may result in lower efficiency in the provision and mix of health care services. That is, public funding does not respond well to consumer preferences (Berger and Messer 2002, p. 2105; Cherney 2003, on-line pages).

3. Private funding, especially through third-party payments, is more likely to support less expensive ambulatory care than in-hospital care. This usually results in healthier outcomes and lower costs of care.

4. If private financing is restricted, support for public funding will decrease (Globerman and Vining 1998). Therefore, increases in private financing will allow public programs to keep within their budget constraints while private funding is allowed to meet unmet health care needs (Broder 2004; Lambert and Healy 2004). This is an important consideration to the United States with respect to its entitlement program for pharmaceutical products. The formulary for these drugs will limit choice and availability.

There have been a number of incidents in the United States that question efficacy when government assumes a role usually reserved for the market participants. In 1993, Hillary Rodham Clinton's Vaccines for Children proposal was approved by Congress. The government bought one-third of the supply of the vaccine at half-price. By 2003, the government was purchasing 55 percent of the vaccine supply. As a result, the number of producers of the vaccine decreased from twenty-five in 1973 to only five in 2003. Moreover, there have been serious shortages of vaccines ("Hillary's Vaccine Shortage" 2003, on-line pages). Clearly, markets will respond to the need for vaccines. If low-income people are unable to pay for the vaccines, then the government may want to provide subsidies. Forced price discounts or price controls will cause shortages. If the supplying firm cannot cover its costs, the supply is simply reduced. There is similar concern for price controls on pharmaceutical drugs.

The following is a summary of the major conclusions reached in this book:

1. The "report cards" issued for managed care were uniformly positive. The managed care organizations (MCOs) reduced the inefficiencies in the system. The rate of inflation for the medical care sector of the consumer price index moderated significantly in the mid-1990s. There was a closer connection between what consumers were willing to pay for and what medical providers were willing to accept (Chapter 4).

2. There is a bold experiment under way in the United States. It is an attempt unlike that in any other nation to envelop markets, government, and institutions in a cooperative venture (Chapter 3).

3. Health savings accounts (HSAs) received generally favorable reviews from the analyses. Some analysts feel that HSAs and other incentive-based plans will lead consumers to invest more in health activities and use more preventative care. The HSAs will promote savings and encourage economizing in the choice of health care services. Others posit that HSAs will crowd out the comprehensive health insurance packages favored by employers and unions. The healthy and the wealthy would leave the comprehensive plans in favor of HSAs. The comprehensive plans would then have higher risk pools. Others found that the nonelderly could reduce their medical expenses by as much as 8 percent with the use of health savings accounts. The HSAs would reduce government tax subsidies that distort economic choices and behavior. The HSA program would be more closely related to the individual needs of consumers (Chapter 6).

4. There is a serious gap in our health care system in the form of over 43 million Americans (2002) without medical insurance. Most studies favor some role for private insurance in any reform proposals. There have been attempts by private, not-for-profit hospitals to provide low-cost or no-cost coverage for the uninsured. Medicaid and Medicare have extended coverage for low-income individuals. We have also seen an extension of insurance coverage through government insurance to chil-

dren, tax credits, and subsidies. Some call for a universal insurance plan (Chapter 5).

5. The Medicare Modernization Act of 2003 sets the stage for a variety of market initiatives designed to promote competition among private insurance firms in the provision of pharmaceutical products. Within the realm of Medicare reform, there is renewed interest in the appropriate roles of government, institutions, and market forces. Chapter 7, on Medicare reform, analyzes these roles and many other issues, including the potential insolvency of the Medicare Trust Fund.

Lessons for Reform: The Policy Implications

1. *Lose the extremes!* In order to create viable policy options, we need to dismiss the extreme positions on the left and the right. The case for a single-buyer, global budget universal health care that is "affordable for all" is nothing more than political babble. It is certainly not politically viable or workable in the dynamic market economy. It would require limitations on the very wants and needs of Americans for the ongoing advances in medicine, technology, and pharmaceutical drugs. Are Americans willing to be dismissed from kidney dialysis when they reach the age of sixty-five or seventy-five? Are they willing to be put on rations for Taxol for breast cancer treatment? Do they want to have their pharmaceutical drug needs eliminated from the formulary list? Probably not. However, these are the trade-offs as we compare and contrast our situation with that of other countries. The right side is not as severe as the left in terms of advocacy of a single answer to the reform question. There does not appear to be a litmus test for inclusion or exclusion of any one criterion. However, the patient power advocates do represent the view of consumer-directed and market-based views for health care reform. The extreme positions "set the table" for health care reform. On the left side, where is our concern for equity in the access, affordability, and distribution of health care services? On the right side, Santa Claus is sure to visit but his helpers need to fill the bag first. Otherwise, there are going to be empty stockings hung and waiting in vain. Market systems promote production and efficiency. They are designed to meet the varying needs and wants of the stocking owners. The wish lists need the transmitting mechanisms of the market. The values (prices), quality, type, and availability are assessed more accurately in the market. Unless the Grinch (monopolist, price

maker, or government) fouls the list. Whose vision and sugar plums dance in whose heads?

2. *Like the in-between positions.* Choose carefully. Look for balance. We conclude, as we did in Chapter 2, in quoting the study by Berger and Messer. They suggested that "as countries increase the level of their health expenditures, they may want to avoid increasing the proportion of their expenditures that are publicly financed" (Berger and Messer 2002, p. 2105[9]).

3. *There is a need for a propitious mix of public and private funding of health care systems.* Public provision, if not production, of health care is designed to provide more equitable access and distribution of health care systems. Private production and provision of health care create economies in purchasing. Markets act to provide more choices and abundance. A market functions to have goods and services valued such that the exchange between buyer and seller might be mutually advantageous or sufficient to make at least one better off and the other not worse off. This facilitates the exchange and adds to efficient outcomes for society. We conclude that given limits to public funding or provision of health care, private financing provides a means to supplement or satisfy the unmet excess demand.

4. *There is a need for public policy that promotes more normal roles for consumers, providers, insurance firms, health care institutions, and firms.* These roles can be supported by appropriate government action to presage and invite changes in the behavior of these participants through provision of subsidies, tax incentives, and cooperative ventures.

We can develop efficient, equitable, and efficacious policies that mix public and private financing if the following conditions are met:

1. Consumers can be enticed to save for medical illnesses and expenses with the use of health savings accounts that receive special tax advantages.
2. Insurance firms can return to their financing functions of underwriting health care policies. This would require these companies to *exclude* coverage for normal or routine expenses such as medical examinations. Insurance would provide coverage for nonroutine and major expenses.
3. Pharmaceutical firms can retain incentives for research. These firms would remain competitive. Government would vigorously enforce anti-trust laws.

Public policy needs to consolidate disease management, clinically based evidence, and reward systems in order to take preemptive steps toward reducing the role of insurance payments for illness care. We might want to consider financing of disease management in preference to the insuring of illness care.

The reimbursement system needs to reward qualitative differences in health outcomes and to require that physicians provide "published evidence of a treatment's effectiveness" (Landro 2003, on-line pages). This is called evidence-based medicine. Health plans are being asked to support programs like the Bridges to Excellence Program, which rewards physicians for successfully monitoring chronic conditions of their patients (Landro 2003, on-line pages).

Future Research

Much of future research will be directed at the evaluation of mixed systems. The Medicare reform legislation of 2003 allows us the opportunity to see how the combined efforts of government, consumers, insurance firms, and medical providers work to provide effective outcomes. As publicly controlled systems seek private financing for unmet or excess demand, and as market-oriented systems look for tax code changes to develop efficiency, we need research to see the convergence possibilities. More international comparisons would afford us the chance to learn even more about other systems. Then we might realize both the limitations and the potential within all systems.

Bibliography

Aaron, Henry J. 1991. *Serious and Unstable Condition.* Washington, DC: Brookings Institution.

———. 1999. "Medicare Choices: Good, Bad, or It All Depends." *Medicare Reform: Issues and Answers,* ed. by Andrew J. Rettenmaier and Thomas R. Saving. Chicago: University of Chicago Press.

Adams, Chris, and Gardiner Harris. 2002. "Drug Makers Face Battle to Preserve Patent Extensions." *Wall Street Journal,* March 19, A24.

Adams, Glenn. 2004. "Maine's Stab at Universal Health Care Taking Shape." *Ithaca Journal,* March 30, 2N.

Anderson, Gerard F., Peter S. Hussey, and Uwe E. Reinhardt. 2004. "US Health Care Spending in an International Context." *Health Affairs* v23, n3 (May/June): 10–25.

Antos, Joseph R., and Linda Bilheimer. 1999. "Medicare Reform: Obstacles and Options." *The American Economic Review* v89, i2 (May): 217–221.

"The Assault on Drug Patents." 2002. *Wall Street Journal,* November 25. http://online.wsj.com (downloaded June 4, 2003).

Baicker, Katherine, and Amitagh Chandra. 2004. "Medicare Spending, the Physician Workforce, and Beneficiaries' Quality of Care." *Health Affairs* 23, no. 3 (May/June): 291.

Baker, Laurence C., and Anne Beeson Royalty. 2000. "Medicaid Policy, Physician Behavior, and Health Care for the Low-Income Population." *Journal of Human Resources* 35, no. 3 (Summer): 480–502.

Bannan, Karen J. 2004. "Is There a Cure?" *My Business* (June/July): 30, 32, 34.

Barth, Sanford M. 2003. "Tackling Rising Health Care Costs." *Government Finance Review* 19, no.1 (February): 32.

Beaulieu, Nancy Dean. 2002. "Quality Information and Consumer Health Plan Choices." *Journal of Health Economics* 21 (2002): 43–63.

Beitia, Arantza. 2003. "Hospital Quality Choice and Market Structure in a Regulated Duopoly." *Journal of Health Economics* 22, no. 6 (November): 1011–1036.

Berenson, Robert A., Jon Christianson, Paul B. Ginsburg, Robert E. Hurley, and Len M. Nichols. 2004. "Are Market Forces Strong Enough to Deliver Efficient Health Care Systems? Confidence Is Waning." *Health Affairs* 23, no. 2 (March/April): 8–21.

Berger, Mark C., and Jodi Messer. 2002. "Public Financing of Health Expenditure, Insurance, and Health Outcomes." *Applied Economics* 34, no. 17 (November): 2105.

Berndt, Ernst R. 1994. "Uniform Pharmaceutical Pricing: An Economic Analysis." *AEI Special Studies in Health Reform.* Washington, DC: AEI Press.

———. 2004. "Perspective: Unique Issues Raised by Drug Benefit Design." *Health Affairs* 23, no. 1 (January/ February): 103–106.

"A Blueprint for New Beginnings." 2004. www.whitehouse.gov (June 8).

Bogner, William C. 1999. "The Pharmaceutical Revolution." *Wall Street Journal,* November 10, A26.

Borlaug, Norman E. 2003. "Science vs. Hysteria." *Wall Street Journal,* January 22, A14.

Breaux, John. 2003. "Curing Health Care: A Universal Solution." *Wall Street Journal,* January 23, A14.

Brock, Fred. 2003. "Why a Centrist (No Fooling) Wants Universal Insurance." *New York Times,* January 5, Bu 7.

Broder, John M. 2004. "Schwarzenegger Budget Denies Some Health Care." *New York Times.* www.nytimes.com (18 January).

Burda, David. 1988. "DRGs." *Modern Healthcare* (4 November): 26–43.

"Business Owners Find Options to Slash Health Insurance Premiums." 2004. (Chart). *My Business* (June/July): 2.

Butler, Stuart M. 2004. "Perspective: A New Policy Framework for Health Care Markets." *Health Affairs* 23, no. 2 (March/April): 22–25.

Calfee, John E. 2000a. *Prices, Markets, and the Pharmaceutical Revolution.* Washington, DC: AEI Press.

———. 2000b. "The Unintended Consequences of Price Controls." *The Economist* (Spring).

Capps, Cory, and David Dranove. 2004. "Marketwatch: Hospital Consolidation and Negotiated PPO Prices." *Health Affairs* 23, no. 2 (March/April) :175–181.

Carlisle, Tamsin. 2003. "Canada Cools to US Drug Flow." *Wall Street Journal.* http://online.wsj.com (26 December).

Carlisle, Tamsin, and Mark Heinzl. 2003. "Canadian Online Pharmacies Vow to Fight Big Drug Markets." *Wall Street Journal.* http://online.wsj.com (12 August).

Carrns, Ann. 2002. "Doctors Treat Uninsured Free of Charge in Project Access." *Wall Street Journal,* December 24, B2, B3.

Chernew, Michael, Richard A. Hirth, Seema S. Sonnad, Rachel Ermann, and A. Mark Fendrick. 1998. "Managed Care, Medical Technology and Health Care Cost Growth: A Review of the Evidence." *Medical Care Research and Review* 55, no. 3 (September): 259–288.

Cherney, Elena. 2003. "Universal Care Has Big Price: Patients Wait." *Wall Street Journal.* http://online.wsj.com (12 November).

"Children in US Managed Care Plans Are Far More Likely to Be Referred to Specialists Than Children in the United Kingdom." *Agency for Healthcare Research and Quality,* July 2003. www.ahrq.gov (downloaded February 11, 2004).

"Choosing to Choose." 2004. *The Economist.* April 10, 45–46.

Clement, Jan P., Vivian Valdmanis, and Kenneth R. White. 2002. "Charity Care: Do Not-for-Profits Influence For-Profits?" *Medical Care Research and Review* 59, no. 1 (March): 59–78.

Cockburn, Iain M. 2004. "The Changing Structure of the Pharmaceutical Industry." *Health Affairs* 23, no. 1 (January/February): 10–22.

Cockburn, Iain, and Zvi Griliches. 1994. "Generics and New Goods in Pharmaceutical Price Indexes." *The American Economic Review* 84, no. 5 (December): 1213–1232.

"A Comeback for MSAs." 2003. *Wall Street Journal.* http://online.wsj.com (June 30).

Cooper, Richard A., and Linda H. Aiken. 2001. "Human Inputs: The Health Care Workforce and Medical Markets." *Journal of Health Politics, Policy and Law Special Issue:* 26, no. 5, *Kenneth Arrow and the Changing Economics of Health Care* (October), ed. Mark A. Peterson, 925–938. Durham, NC: Duke University Press.

Culter, David M., and Louise Sheiner. 1999. "The Geography of Medicare." In *The American Economic Review* 89, no. 2 (May): 228–233.

Cunningham, Peter J., Jack Hadley, and James Reschovsky. 2002. "The Effects of SCHIP on Children's Health Insurance Coverage: Early Evidence from the Community Tracking Study." *Medical Care Research and Review* 59, no. 4 (December): 359–383.

Cutler, David M., ed. 2000. *The Changing Hospital Industry: Comparing Not-for-Profit and For-Profit Institutions.* Chicago: University of Chicago Press.

———. 2002. "Equality, Efficiency, and Market Fundamentals: The Dynamics of International Medical-Care Reform." *Journal of Economic Literature* 40 (September): 881–906.

"Cut Out the Costly Co-Pays with Affordable HSAs." 2004. *My Business* (August/September): 46.

Danzon, Patricia M. 1994. "Global Budgets Versus Competitive Cost-Control Strategies." *AEI Special Studies in Health Reform.* Washington, DC: AEI Press.

———. 1999. "Price Comparison for Pharmaceuticals: A Review of US and Cross-National Studies." *AEI Special Studies.* Washington, DC: AEI Press.

Danzon, Patricia, Paul J. Feldstein, John Hoff, and Mark V. Pauly. 1992. *Responsible National Insurance.* Washington, DC: AEI Press.

Davis, Erin, and Richard Kaglie. 2002. "Reining in Medicaid Spending—States Respond to Declining Revenues." *Chicago Fed Letter,* no. 175 (March). Chicago, IL: The Federal Reserve Bank of Chicago.

Davis, Karen. 1975. *National Health Insurance: Benefits, Costs, and Consequences.* Washington, DC: Brookings Institution.

———. 2003. Commentary. *Medical Care Research and Review* 60, Supplement to 60, no. 2 (June): 89S–99S.

Davis, Karen, Michelle Doty, Cathy Schoen, and Katie Tenney. 2002. "Medicare Versus Private Insurance: Rhetoric and Reality." *Health Affairs Web Exclusive,* October 9, w311–w312.

DeScherer, Dorinda D., and Terence M. Myers. 2004. *Employee Benefits Answer Book.* 8th ed. New York: Aspen Publishers.

"Detroit's Health-Care Tar Pit." 2003. *Wall Street Journal.* http://online.wsj.com (July 18).

Dranove, David. 2002. *The Economic Evolution of American Health Care.* Princeton: Princeton University Press.

———. 2003. *What's Your Life Worth? Health Care Rationing . . . Who Lives? Who Dies? Who Decides?* New York: Prentice Hall.

Dranove, David and William D. White. 1999. "How Hospitals Survived: Competition and the American Hospital." *AEI Special Studies in Health Reform.* Washington DC: AEI Press.

Dreazen, Yochi, Grag Ip, and Nicholas Kulish. 2002. "Why the Sudden Rise in the Urge to Merge and Form Oligopolies," and "Merger Wave." *Wall Street Journal,* February 25, 1, 10.

"Drug-Price Program Notes." 2000. *Wall Street Journal,* August 10, A18.

"Drug Wars." 2004. *Wall Street Journal,* April 26, A14.

Enthoven, Alain C. 2004. "Perspective: Market Forces and Efficiency Health Care Systems." *Health Affairs* 23, no. 2 (March/April): 25–27.

Evans, Robert G. "Going for the Gold: The Redistributive Agenda Behind Market-based Health Care Reform." *Healthy Markets? The New Competition in Medical Care,* ed. Mark A Peterson, 66–109. Durham, NC: Duke University Press.

Feldman, Roger D., ed. 2000. *American Health Care.* New Brunswick: Transaction.

Feldstein, Martin. 1999. "Prefunding Medicare." *AEA Papers and Proceedings* 89, no. 2 (May): 222–227.

———. 2003. "Health and Taxes." *Wall Street Journal,* January 19, A13.

"Fee-for-Service Medicare Plans Offer Better Quality Care than Medicare HMO Plans, but Costs are Higher." 2002. *Agency for Healthcare Research and Quality,* July. www.ahrq.gov (downloaded February 11).

Findlay, Steven, and Joel Miller. 1999. "Down a Dangerous Path: The Erosion of Health Insurance Coverage in the United States." May. *Policy Studies.* www.americashealth.org (downloaded June 15).

Finkelstein, Katherine E. 2001. "Celebrated Hospital Merger a Union in Name Only." *New York Times,* December 2.

"Fistfuls of Health Dollars." 2004. *The Economist,* June 5, 33–34.

Fogarty, Thomas A. 2003. "Investors Find Shelter in Health Accounts." *Ithaca Journal,* December 25, A6.

Frank, Robert, and Scott Hensley. 2002. "Pfizer to Buy Pharmacia for $60 Billion." *Wall Street Journal,* July 15, A1, A6.

Frean, Alexandra. 2000. "Doctors and Dentists Told to 'Open All Hours.'" *London Times,* March 10, 8.

Frech, H.E. III, and Richard D. Millar, Jr. 1999. "The Productivity of Health Care and Pharmaceuticals: An International Comparison." *AEI Special Studies.* Washington, DC: AEI Press.

Freudenheim, Milt. 1999. "Big H.M.O. to Give Decisions on Care Back to Doctors." *New York Times.* www.nytimes.com (November 9).

———. 2000a. "Aetna Plans a Recovery; HMO's May Not Make It." *New York Times,* March 19, B4.

———. 2000b. " 'Buyers' Clubs' for Medical Services Crop Up." *New York Times,* August 25, A2, C19.

———. 2002. "As Drug Patents End, Costs for Generics Surge." *New York Times,* December 27. www.nytimes.com (downloaded January 2).

———. 2003a. "Employers Seek to Shift Costs of Drugs to US." *New York Times,* www.nytimes.com (July 2).

———. 2003b. "Growth in Drug Spending Slows." *New York Times,* June 3. www.nytimes.com (downloaded June 4).

Friedman, Milton. 2001. "How to Cure Health Care." *Hoover Digest* no. 3: 40–55.

Fuhrmans, Vanessa. 2004a. "Attacking Rise in Health Costs, Big Company Meets Resistance." *Wall Street Journal.* http://online.wsj.com (July 13).

————. 2004b. "Health Premiums Grow More Slowly Than Expected." *Wall Street Journal.* http://online.wsj.com (June 21).

Gaynor, Martin, and Deborah Haas-Wilson. 1999. "Change, Consolidation, and Competition in Health Care Markets." *Journal of Economic Perspectives* 13, no. 1 (Winter): 141–164.

Gaynor, Martin, Deborah Haas-Wilson, and William B. Vogt. 2000. "Are Invisible Hands Good Hands? Moral Hazard, Competition, and the Second-Best in Health Care Markets." *Journal of Political Economy* 108, no. 5 (October): 992–1005.

Gelijns, Annetine C., Richard R. Nelson, and Joshua Graff Zivin. 2001. "Uncertainty and Technological Change in Medicine." *Journal of Health Politics, Policy and Law Special Issue:* 26, no. 5, *Kenneth Arrow and the Changing Economics of Health Care* (October), ed. Mark A. Peterson, 913–924. Durham, NC: Duke University Press.

Glied, Sherry A. 2001. "Health Insurance and Market Failure Since Arrow." *Journal of Health Politics, Policy and Law Special Issue:* 26, no. 5, *Kenneth Arrow and the Changing Economics of Health Care* (October), ed. Mark A. Peterson, 957–966. Durham, NC: Duke University Press.

————. 2003. "Health Care Costs: On the Rise Again." *Journal of Economic Perspectives* 17, no. 2 (Spring): 125–148.

Globerman, Steven, and Aidan Vining. 1998. "A Policy Perspective on 'Mixed' Health Care Financial Systems of Business and Economics." *The Journal of Risk and Insurance* 65, no. 1 (March): 57–80.

Goldman, Dana P., Joan L. Buchanan, and Emmett B. Keeler. 2000. "Simulating the Impact of Medical Savings Accounts on Small Business." *Health Services Research* 35, no. 1, Part 1 (April): 53–75.

Goldman, Dana P., Geoffrey F. Joyce, and Jesse D. Malkin. 2004. "From the Field: The Changing Force of Pharmacy Benefit Design." *Health Affairs* 23, no. 1 (January/February): 194–199.

Goodman, John C. 2003. "A Better Fix for Medicare." *Wall Street Journal,* June 27, A12.

Goodman, John C., and Gerald L. Musgrave. 1992. *Patient Power: Solving America's Health Care Crisis.* Washington, DC: Cato Institute.

Gratzer, David. 2003. "How Not to Handle Health Care." *Wall Street Journal.* http://online.wsj.com (October 1).

Greenberg, Lisa. 2001. "Overview: PPO Performance Measurement: Agenda for the Future." *Medical Care Research and Review* 58, Supplement 1: 8–15.

Gross, Daniel. 2004. "Whose Problem Is Health Care?" *New York Times,* February 8, B6.

Gruber, Jonathan. 2003. "Evaluating Alternative Approaches to Incremental Health Insurance Expansion." *AEA Papers and Proceedings* 93, no. 2 (May): 271–276.

Haas-Wilson, Deborah. 2003. *Managed Care and Monopoly Power: The Antitrust Challenge.* Cambridge, MA: Harvard University Press.

Hadley, Jack. 2003. "Sicker and Poorer—The Consequences of Being Uninsured: A Review of the Research on the Relationship Between Health Insurance, Medical Care Use, Health, Work, and Income." *Medical Care Research and Review* 60, no. 2 (June): 3S-75S.

Hall, Mark A. 1994. *Reforming Private Health Insurance.* Washington, DC: AEI Press.

Harris, Gardiner. 2003. "If Americans Want to Pay Less for Drugs, They Will." *New York Times*. www.nytimes.com (November 16).

Hawkins, Lee Jr. 2005. "Doctors Fight Insurer's Cuts to Auto Workers." *Wall Street Journal*, February 8, B1, B6.

Health Affairs. 2004. Bethesda, MD: Published by Project Hope, 23, no. 4 (July/August).

Health Policy Alternatives Inc. 2004. "Prescription Drug Coverage for Medicare Beneficiaries: An Overview of the Medicare Prescription Drug, Improvement, and Modernization Act of 2003." January 14. The Kaiser Family Foundation.

"Healthy Habits." 2004. *My Business* (June/July). National Federation of Independent Business (NFIB).

Heffley, Dennis R. and Thomas J. Miceli. 1998. "The Economics of Incentive-based Health Care Plans." *Journal of Risk and Insurance* 65, no. 3 (September): 445–465.

Henderson, James W. 2002. *Health Economics and Policy*. 2nd ed. Cincinnati, OH: South-Western Publishers.

Hensley, Scott. 2002a. "Doctors Aren't Immune to Pitches by Drug Firms." *Wall Street Journal*. http://online.wsj.com (December 11).

———. 2002b. "How New Generics Can Cut Your Drug Bills." *Wall Street Journal*, June 6, D1, D3.

———. 2002c. "Pfizer Hawks Discount-Drug Card." *Wall Street Journal*. http://online.wsj.com (December 17).

———. 2003a. "Managers of Drug Plans Face an Uncertain Role." *Wall Street Journal*. http://online.wsj.com (July 11).

———. 2003b. "Sales Battles by Pfizer, Others Begin to Wane, But Few Dare to Retreat." *Wall Street Journal Europe*, June 13–15, A1, A6.

———. 2004. "Medicare Move Likely to Benefit Costliest Drugs." *Wall Street Journal*, February 24, B1, B6.

Hernandez, Raymond, and Al Baker. 2005. "Bush's Proposals Could Lead to Overhaul in State Medicaid." *New York Times*, January 9, N23, N28.

"Hillary Care in Tennessee." 2004. *Wall Street Journal*, December 6, A14.

"Hillary's Vaccine Shortage." 2003. *Wall Street Journal*. http://online.wsj.com (August 15).

Hobijn, Bart, and David Lagakos. 2003. "Social Security and the Consumer Price Index for the Elderly." *Current Issues in Economics and Finance* (May). New York: Federal Reserve Bank of New York. www.ny.frb.org/research/currentissues/ci9–5/ci9–5.html.

Ingebretsen, Mark. 2003. "US Facing a Nursing Shortage." *Wall Street Journal*. http://online.wsj.com (November 14).

———. 2004. "Attention Is Refocusing on Universal Health Care." *Wall Street Journal*. http://online.wsj.com (January 16).

Inside Consumer-Directed Care. 2004. 2, no. 9 (May).

Institute of Medicine. 2004. "Insuring America's Health: Principles and Recommendations." January. Washington, DC: National Academies Press.

Jacobson, Peter D. 2001. "Regulating Health Care: From Self-Regulation to Self-Regulation?" *Journal of Health Politics, Policy and Law Special Issue:* 26, no. 5, *Kenneth Arrow and the Changing Economics of Health Care* (October), ed. Mark A. Peterson, 1165–1178. Durham, NC: Duke University Press.

Jensen, Gail A. 2000. "Making Room for Medical Saving Accounts in the US Health Care System." *American Health Care,* ed. Roger D. Feldman. Oakland, CA: The Independent Institute.

Johannes, Laura, and Rachel Zimmerman. 2000. "SmithKline Move in Maine Signals Battle over Prices." *Wall Street Journal.* http://online.wsj.com (August 15).

Johnson, Everett A., Montague Brown, and Richard L. Johnson. 1996. *The Economic Era of Health Care: A Revolution in Organized Delivery Systems.* San Francisco, CA: Jossey-Bass.

Johnson, Richard W., and Stephen Crystal. 2000. "Uninsured Status and Out-of-Pocket Costs at Midlife." *Health Services Research* 35, no. 5, Part 1 (December): 911–930.

Johnston, David Cay. 2004. "Nonprofit Hospital Agrees to Limits on Patient Fees." *New York Times.* www.nytimes.com (August 6).

Kaestner, Robert, and Neeraj Kaushal. 2003. "Welfare Reform and Health Insurance Coverage of Low-Income Families." *Journal of Health Economics* 22, no. 6 (November): 959–981.

The Kaiser Family Foundation. 2004a. "Medicare Fact Sheet." Washington DC: The Kaiser Family Foundation and Hewitt, 1–2.

———. 2004b. *Retiree Health Benefits Now and in the Future.* Washington, DC: The Kaiser Family Foundation and Hewitt.

Kendix, Michael, and James D. Lubitz. 1999. "The Impact of Medical Savings Accounts on Medicare Program Costs." *Inquiry* 36 (Fall): 280–290.

Kifman, Mathias. 2002. "Community Rating in Health Insurance and Different Benefit Packages." *Journal of Health Economics* 21, no. 5: 719–737.

Kirland, Kerry, Michelle Kitchman, Frank B. McArdle, Patricia Neuman, and Dale Yamamoto. 2004. "Large Firms' Retiree Health Benefits Before Medicare Reform: 2003 Survey Results." *Health Affairs* 23, no. 2 (March/April): 289.

Kobliner, Beth. 2003. "A New Health Plan Works, at Least for the Healthy." *New York Times,* March 2, Bu 8.

Kolata, Gina. 2002. "Research Suggests More Health Care May Not Be Better." *New York Times.* www.nytimes.com (July 21).

Lagnado, Lucette. 2003a. "Hospitals Will Give Price Breaks to Uninsured, if Medicare Agrees." *Wall Street Journal.* http://online.wsj.com (December 17).

———. 2003b. "One Critical Appendectomy Later, Young Woman Has a $19,000 Debt." *Wall Street Journal.* http://online.wsj.com (March 17).

———. 2003c. "Taming Hospital Billing: Lawmakers Push Legislation to Curb Aggressive Collection Against Uninsured Patients." *Wall Street Journal,* June 10, B2, B6.

Lambert, Bruce, and Patrick Healy. 2004. "At 2 Hospitals, Fiscal Troubles in the Glare of Public View." *New York Times.* www.nytimes.com (January 18).

Landers, Peter. 2002. "Medicare Plans to Reward HMOs Treating Sickest Patients." *Wall Street Journal,* February 20, B1, B10.

———. 2003. "Medicare Will Pay Insurers More to Take Sicker Patients." *Wall Street Journal.* http://online.wsj.com (December 30).

———. 2004. "Method Actors: In Drug Market . . . Surprising Role." *Wall Street Journal,* May 10, A1, A11.

Landro, Laura. 2003. "Six Prescriptions to Ease Rationing US Health Care." *Wall Street Journal.* http://online.wsj.com (December 22).

Langone, John. 2003. "The Shapers of Health Care." *New York Times.* www.nytimes.com (July 8).

Lee, Susan. 2004. "A Tax-Code Cure for Ailing Health Care." *Wall Street Journal,* August 9, A13.

Lemieux, Pierre. 2004. "Canada's 'Free' Health Care Has Hidden Costs." 2004. *Wall Street Journal,* April 23, A15.

Levit, Katherine, Cynthia Smith, Cathy Cowman, Art Sensenig, Aaron Catlin, and the Health Accounts Team. 2004. "Trends: Health Spending Rebound Continues in 2002." *Health Affairs,* 23, no. 1 (January/February): 147–159.

Lichtenberg, Frank R. 2002. "The Effects of Medicare on Health Care Utilization and Outcomes." *Frontiers in Health Policy Research,* ed. Alan M. Garber, 27–52. Cambridge, MA: National Bureau of Economic Research.

Lieber, Ron. 2004. "New Way to Curb Medical Costs: Make Employees Feel the Sting." *Wall Street Journal.* http://online.wsj.com (June 23).

Lubitz, James, Liming Cai, Ellen Kramarow, and Harold Lentzner. 2003. "Health, Life Expectancy, and Health Care Among the Elderly." *New England Journal of Medicine* 349, no. 11 (September 11): 1048–1055.

Lueck, Sarah. 2003. "Medicare Law Reaches the Under-65 Set, Too." *Wall Street Journal,* December 11, D1.

———. 2004. "Medicare-Participant Plans to Get $500 Millions in Funds This Year." *Wall Street Journal,* January 16. http://online.wsj.com (downloaded January 18).

Lueck, Sarah, and Jacob M. Schlesinger. 2003. "AARP Backs Prescription Deal." *Wall Street Journal.* http://online.wsj.com (November 18).

McClellan, Mark, and Jonathan Skinner. 1999. "Medicare Reform: Who Pays and Who Benefits?" *Health Affairs* 18, no. 1 (January/February): 48–62.

McGinley, Laurie. 2004. "Health Club: Behind Medicare's Decisions, an Invisible Web of Gatekeepers." *Wall Street Journal,* September 16. http://online.wsj.com (downloaded September 17).

McGinley, Laurie, and Sarah Lueck. 2003. "Behind Drug-Benefit Debate: How to Mix Medicare, Markets." *Wall Street Journal.* http://online.wsj.com (November 17).

Magleby, James E. 1996. "Hospital Mergers and Antitrust Policy: Arguments Against a Modification of Current Antitrust Law." *Antitrust Bulletin* 41, no. 1 (Spring): 137–201.

Martin, Cathie Jo. 1998. "Markets, Medicare and Making Do: Business Strategies After National Health Care Reform." *Health Markets? The New Competition in Medicare Care,* ed. Mark A. Peterson, 223–254. Durham/London: Duke University Press.

Martinez, Barbara. 2002. "After an Era of Dominant HMOs, Hospitals Are Turning the Tables." *Wall Street Journal.* http://online.wsj.com (April 12).

———. 2003a. "Rate of Increase for Health Costs May Be Slowing." *Wall Street Journal,* June 11, A1, A12.

———. 2003b. "With Medical Costs Climbing, Workers Are Asked to Pay More." *Wall Street Journal,* June 16, A1, A6.

Mathews, Anna Wilde. 2003. "States to Help Citizens Import Canadian Drugs." 2003. *Wall Street Journal,* December 18, B1, B6.

Matthews, Merrill, Jr. 2002. "On a Bus to Bangor, Canadians Seeking Health Care." *Wall Street Journal,* July 6, A13.

Medical Society of the District of Columbia. 1984. *Physician's Reference Guide 4.* Washington, DC: Medical Society of The District of Columbia.

"Medicare." 2001. *Social Security Bulletin. Annual Statistical Supplement 2001.* 5, 43–62.

———. 2003. *Social Security Bulletin. Annual Statistical Supplement 2003.* 4, 33–44.

Melnick, Glenn, Emmett Keeler, and Jack Zwanziger. 1999. "Market Power and Hospital Pricing: Are Non-profits Different?" *Health Affairs* 18, no. 3 (May/June): 167–173.

Miller, James. 2000. "Genetic Testing and Health Insurance." *The Dismal Scientist,* August 17. www.dismal.com (September 12).

Miller, Robert H. 1996. "Competition in the Health System: Good News and Bad News." *Health Affairs* 15, no. 2 (Summer): 107–120.

Miller, Wilhelmine, Elizabeth Richardson Vigdor, and Willard G. Manning. 2004. "Covering the Uninsured: What Is It Worth?" *Health Affairs* 23, no. 3 (May/June): 290.

MMA Summary 2004. www.medicare.gov.

Morrisey, Michael A., ed. 1998. *Managed Care and Changing Health Care Markets.* Washington, DC: AEI Press.

Morton, Fiona Scott. 1997. "The Strategic Response by Pharmaceutical Firms to the Medicaid Most-Favored-Customer Rules." *The RAND Journal of Economics* 28, no. 2 (Summer): 269–290.

Murray, Alan. 2003. "Medicare Drug Plan Is an Experiment Well Worth Making." *Wall Street Journal.* http://online.wsj.com (November 18).

Nano, Stephanie. 2003. "Study Unveils Drop in Medication Use When Co-Pays Jump." *Ithaca Journal,* December 4, A1, A4.

Needleman, Jack. 2001. "The Role of Nonprofits in Health Care." *Journal of Health Politics, Policy and Law Special Issue:* 26, no. 5, *Kenneth Arrow and the Changing Economics of Health Care* (October), ed. Mark A. Peterson, 1113–1130. Durham, NC: Duke University Press.

Newhouse, Joseph P. 1992. "Medical Care Costs: How Much Welfare Loss?" *Journal of Economic Perspectives* 6, no. 3 (Summer): 3–21.

———. 2002. *Pricing the Priceless: A Health Care Conundrum.* Cambridge, MA: National Bureau of Economic Research.

———. 2004. "How Much Should Medicare Pay for Drugs?" *Health Affairs* 23, no. 1 (January/February): 89–102. Bethesda, MD: Project Hope.

"The New York Health Care Reform Act and What It Means to You." 1977. *Health Visions* (Winter). Cayuga Medical Center.

Organization for Economic Co-Operation and Development (OECD). 2001. *Health at a Glance.* Paris: OECD.

———. 2002. *OECD Health Data 2002.* Paris: OECD.

———. 2003a. "Across the Border." (Chart). *Wall Street Journal.* http://online.wsj.com (November 12).

———. 2003b. *Health at a Glance.* OECD Indicators. Paris. OECD.

"Overview: Dirigo Health." 2003. *Maine.gov.* www.state.me.us/gov (July 7).

Ozanne, Larry. 1996. "How Will Medical Savings Accounts Affect Medical Spending?" *Inquiry* 33 (Fall): 225–236.

Pammolli, Fabio, and Massimo Riccaboni. 2004. "Perspective: Market Structure and Drug Innovation." *Health Affairs* 23, no. 1 (January/February): 48–50.

Pauly, Mark V. 1994. "An Analysis of Medical Savings Accounts: Do Two Wrongs Make a Right?" *AEI Special Studies in Health Reform.* Washington, DC: AEI Press.

———. 2000. *Health Benefits at Work.* Ann Arbor: University of Michigan Press.

———. 2001. "Forward." *Journal of Health Policies, Policy and Law.* Special Issue 26, no. 5 (October).

———. 2004. "Medicare Drug Coverage and Moral Hazard." *Health Affairs* 23, no. 1 (January/February): 113–122.

Pavcnik, Nina. 2002. "Do Pharmaceutical Prices Respond to Potential Patient Out-of-Pocket Expenses?" *The RAND Journal of Economics* 33, no. 3 (Autumn). OCLC Firstsearch. Article BBPI02155391. http://firstsearch.oclc.org (downloaded June 11).

"Pharmacists Offer Drug-Discount Card as Rival to PBM's" 2004. *Wall Street Journal,* June 16, B1, B6.

Pollock, Robert L. 2003a. "Americans Need a Market for Medical Progress." *Wall Street Journal,* January 22, A14.

———. 2003b. "Curing Health Care." *Wall Street Journal,* January 22, A14.

Powell, Philip T., and David Nakata. 2001. "Can Earnings Decline Cause a Retirement Flight of Physicians? Financial Compensation and the Decision to Stay in Practice." *Medical Care Research and Review* 58, no. 3 (September): 361–378.

"The Reform of Health Care Systems: A Review of Seventeen OECD Countries." 1994. *Health Policy Studies,* no. 5. Paris: 45–50.

Reinhardt, Uwe E. 2001. "Can Efficiency in Health Care Be Left to the Market?" *Journal of Health Politics, Policy and Law Special Issue:* 26, no. 5, *Kenneth Arrow and the Changing Economics of Health Care* (October), ed. Mark A. Peterson, 967–922. Durham, NC: Duke University Press.

———. 2004. "Perspective: An Information Infrastructure for the Pharmaceutical Market." *Health Affairs* 23, no. 1 (January/February): 107–112.

"Report on Feasibility." 2003. Illinois Department of Central Management. www.house.gov/burton/rxff_4.htm. (October 27).

"Report Says Medicare to Go Broke by 2019." 2004. *Road Runner News.* www.rr.com/flash/browser.cfm?div_id=43&debug=0 (March 23).

Rettenmaier, Andrew J., and Thomas R. Saving, eds. 1999. *Medicare Reform: Issues and Answers.* Chicago: University of Chicago Press.

———. 2000. *The Economics of Medicare Reform.* Kalamazoo, MI: W.E. Upjohn Institute for Employment Research.

Rhoades, Jeffrey A., Joel Cohen, and Jessica P. Vistnes. 2003. "Chartbook #9: The Uninsured in America: 1996–2000." *Medical Expenditure Panel Survey,* April. Agency for Healthcare Research and Quality. http://meps.ahrq.gov (downloaded June 11).

Rice, Thomas. 1998. "Can Markets Give Us the Health System We Want?" *The New Competition in Medical Care,* ed. Mark A. Peterson, 27–65. Durham, NC: Duke University Press.

Riemer, David R. 1990. "Milwaukee's Successful Effort to Control Employee Health Care Costs." *Government Finance Review* 6, no. 1 (February): 15–17.

"Rising Medical Costs Can Be a Good Thing." 2001. *Wall Street Journal.* http://online.wsj.com (July 26).

Robinson, James C., and Jill M. Yegian. 2004. "Medical Management After Managed Care." *Health Affairs* 10 (May). http://content.healthaffairs.org (May 25).

Rogers, Lois. 2000. "NHS Spends £450m on Private Treatment." *London Times*, March 5, 2.

Rosko, Michael D. 2001. "Impact of HMO Penetration and Other Environmental Factors on X-Inefficiency." *Medical Care Research and Review* 58, no. 4 (December): 430–434.

Rundle, Rhonda L. 2003. "Pay-As-You-Go M.D.: The Doctor Is In, But Insurance Is Out." *Wall Street Journal*, November 6. http://online.wsj.com (downloaded December 17).

Santerre, Rexford E., and Stephen P. Neun. 1996. *Health Economics: Theories, Insights, and Industry Studies*. Boston: Irwin.

———. 2000. *Health Economics: Theories, Insights, and Industry Study*. Rev. ed. New York: Dryden Press.

Scherer, F.M. 1993. "Pricing, Profits, and Technological Progress in the Pharmaceutical Industry." *Journal of Economic Perspectives* 7, no. 3 (Summer): 97–115.

Schumann, Laurence, and Michael G. Vita. 1991. "The Competitive Effects of Horizontal Mergers in the Hospital Industry: A Closer Look." *Journal of Health Economics* 10, no. 3 (October): 359–372.

Slater, Joanna. 2003. "Health Drug Makers Emerge as Important Rivals." *Wall Street Journal*. http://online.wsj.com (November 13).

Sloan, Frank A. 2002. "Hospital Ownership Conversions: Defining the Appropriate Public Oversight Role." *Frontiers in Health Policy Research*, ed. Alan M. Garber, 123–166. Cambridge, MA: National Bureau of Economic Research.

Smith, Cynthia. 2004. "Trends: Retail Prescription Drug Spending in the National Health Accounts." *Health Affairs* 23, no. 1 (January/February): 160–167.

Smith, David. 2000. "The Cure: Saving the NHS." *Sunday London Times*, March 5, 6.

Smith, Peter C., and Nick York. 2004. "Quality Incentives: The Case of UK General Practitioners." *Health Affairs* 23, no. 3 (May/June): 112–118.

Snow, John W. 2005. "Statement on the 2005 Social Security and Medicare Trust Fund Reports." March 23. www.treas.gov.

Solomon, Jay. 2004. "India's New Group in Outsourcing: Inpatient Care." *Wall Street Journal*. http://online.wsj.com (April 26).

"States of Recovery." 2003. *Wall Street Journal*, December 3, A16.

"States Use Their Purchasing Power as Leverage to Limit Drug Prices." 2002. *Wall Street Journal*. http://online.wsj.com (September 13).

Stolberg, Sheryl Gay, and Jeff Gerth. 2000a. "Drug Companies Profit from Research Supported by Taxpayers." *New York Times*, April 23. www.nytimes.com (downloaded August 16).

———. 2000b. "How Companies Stall Generics and Keep Themselves Healthy." *New York Times*, July 23. www.nytimes.com (downloaded August 16).

———. 2000c. "In a Drug's Journey to Market, Discovery Is Just the First of Many Steps." *New York Times*, July 23. www.nytimes.com (downloaded August 16).

Strom, Stephanie. 2003. "For Middle Class, Health Insurance Becomes a Luxury." *New York Times*, November 16. www.nytimes.com.

Strunk, Bradley C., and Peter J. Cunningham. 2002. "Treading Water: Americans'

Access to Needed Medical Care, 1997–2001." *Medical Benefits*, no. 1 (April): 5–6.

Stuart, Bruce, Puneet K. Singhal, Cheryl Fahlman, Jalpa Doshi, and Becky Briesacher. 2003. "Employer-Sponsored Health Insurance and Prescription Drug Coverage for New Retirees: Dramatic Declines in Five Years." *Health Affairs Web Exclusives*, (July 23): W3–W334.

Sultz, Harry A., and Kristina M. Young. 2004. *Health Care USA: Understanding Its Organization and Delivery,* 4th ed. Boston: Jones and Bartlett.

"Supreme Court Rx." 2003. *Wall Street Journal.* http://online.wsj.com. (May 21).

"Sure, Cheap Canadian Drugs." 2002. *Wall Street Journal*, July 23, A14.

Tai-Seale, Ming, and Gerard J. Wedig. 2002. "The Effect of Report Cards on Consumer Choice in the Health Insurance Market." *Journal of Health Economics* 21, no. 6 (November): 1031–1048.

"Teddy's Nightmare." 2003. *Wall Street Journal.* http://online.wsj.com. (December 23).

Tengs, Tammy O., Miriam E. Adams, Joseph S. Pliskin, Dana Gelb Safran, Joanna E. Siegel, Milton C. Weinstein, and John D. Graham, 1995. "Five-Hundred Life-Saving Interventions and Their Cost-Effectiveness." *Risk Analysis* 15, no. 3: 370–389.

"Three Major Health Care Providers Quit Several Big Medicare Markets." 2000. *Wall Street Journal.* http://online.wsj.com (June 29).

U.S. Department of Health and Human Services. Centers for Medicare and Medicaid Services. 2004. "The Facts About Upcoming New Benefits in Medicare." February 17. United States: Department of Health and Human Services.

———. 2005. "Medicare and You." Baltimore: U.S. DHS.

U.S. Department of the Treasury. 2003. "21ˢᵗ Century Medicare." www.treas.gov.

———. 2004a. "About HSAs." www.treas.gov (June 8).

———. 2004b. "HSA Frequently Asked Questions." www.treas.gov (June 8).

U.S. House of Representatives. Ways and Means Committee. 2003. "Appendix C—National and International Health Care Expenditures and Health Insurance." http://waysandmeans.house.gov/greenbook.

Vernon, J.A. 2005. "Examining the Link Between Price Regulation and Pharmaceutical R&D Investment." *Health Economics* 14, no. 1: 1–16.

"A Victory for Private Medicine." 1999. *Wall Street Journal*, July 29, A26.

Waldholz, Michael. 2002. "States Use their Purchasing Power as Leverage to Limit Drug Prices." *Wall Street Journal*, July 21. http://online.wsj .com (downloaded September 13).

———. 2003. "Medicare Clause Could Help Very Ill While Cutting Costs." *Wall Street Journal*, July 30. http://online.wsj.com (downloaded July 9).

Weisbrod, Burton A. 1991. "The Health Care Quadrilemma: An Essay on Technological Changes, Insurance, Quality of Care, and Cost Containment." *Journal of Economic Literature,* 29 (June): 523–552.

Wennberg, John E., Elliot S. Fisher, and Jonathan S. Skinner. 2002. "Geography and the Debate Over Medicare Reform." *Health Affairs Web Exclusives* (February): W96–W114.

Wessel, David. 2003. "Americans Are Buying Even More Health Care." *Wall Street Journal*, January 9, A2.

Whitener, Mark D. 2003. "Anti-Trust, Medicare Reform and Health Care Competition." *American Enterprise Institute for Policy Research.* www.ftc.gov/speeches/other/whisp.htm

"Why Drug Prices Keep Soaring." 2002. *Wall Street Journal*. http://online.wsj.com (September 12).

"Why You Can't Buy Insurance." 2002. *Wall Street Journal*. http://online.wsj.com (October 1).

Winslow, Ron. 2002. "Unusual Disease-Care Plan to be Unveiled by Blue Cross and American Healthways." *Wall Street Journal*. http://online.wsj.com (December 10).

Wooley, J. Michael. 1991. "The Competitive Effects of Horizontal Mergers in the Hospital Industry: An Even Closer Look." *Journal of Health Economics* 10: 373–378.

Wysocki, Bernard, Jr. 2003. "Tomorrow's Elderly Fuel Health-Care Spending and Strain the System." *Wall Street Journal*. http://online.wsj.com (December 29).

Yanchunas, Dom. 2003. "The Allure of Canada's Low Prices." *Binghamton Press and Sun Bulletin*, December 28. A1, A13.

Zabinski, Daniel, Thomas M. Selden, John F. Moeller, and Jessica S. Banthin. 1999. "Medical Savings Accounts: Micro Simulation Results from a Model with Adverse Selection." *Journal of Health Economics* 18: 195–218.

Zhou, Huizhong, ed. 2001. *The Political Economy of Health Care Reforms*. Kalamazoo, MI: W. E. Upjohn Institute for Employment Research.

Index